If You Plant It They Will Come

A Butterfly Habitat Creation Success Story

Christopher Kline

Butterfly Ridge Butterfly Conservation Center ltd.
17864 State Route 374
Rockbridge, Ohio 43149
www.butterfly-ridge.com

ISBN-13: 978-1734619706

Table of Contents

Introduction

As a child growing up in suburban Dayton, Ohio, I enjoyed catching insects and watching them. Most of my efforts were directed at butterflies and grasshoppers. While I thought the butterflies were pretty and interesting, the grasshoppers were my favorites.

When I would capture these wonderful insects, the butterflies would go into a glass jar with holes punched in the lid. And usually they would eventually die in these jars, and for that I apologize. Nobody taught me the importance of providing nectar for my prisoners. Whether they would've partaken of nectar in the small cell I provided is anybody's guess.

The grasshoppers would go into metal coffee cans with plastic lids. I very much enjoyed the drumming sounds that the grasshoppers would make as they hopped and hit the lid of the can. Hence the reason they were my favorite.

As I entered adulthood, my interest in insects remained, but took on a different form. No longer were metal coffee cans my field tool of choice. The fact that coffee isn't packaged in metal cans anymore, or that nobody in my adult home drinks coffee, has had no influence on my collection habits. My tools of choice are now my camera, chain saw, and shovel. The coffee can prison has been replaced by a tall grass Shangri La.

Which brings us to the point of this book. Starting in the early 2000's, most news reports about pollinators, and butterflies specifically, have been doom-and-gloom. The butterfly sky has been falling for nearly two decades. It would seem that Chicken Little has been reincarnated as a lepidopterist. If one were to listen to the news, butterfly-themed listservs, and butterfly Facebook pages, all butterflies are well on their way to extinction.

While the populations of some butterflies are definitely in a long-term decline, to use the e-word is alarmist and premature. However, since it is used with such impunity, many butterfly watchers and hobbyists are believing the paranoid declarations of the end of the four-winged world.

The very thing that could reverse the negative trends in butterfly population dynamics is the very thing that is not being talked about. The 'experts' spend so much time bashing and litigating against herbicide and pesticide manufacturers, butterfly breeders, and grandmothers raising butterflies with their grandchildren in their backyards, that they are missing the most obvious tool to help our winged friends re-establish their footing; education.

This book is an attempt to provide that education. This book is a 'How To' success story. It is hard to say whether this publication will gain traction in media reporting, since it goes against the gloom-and-doom trend. However, if you want to benefit the butterflies, and other pollinators, in your local community, this book, tweaked to fit your local environment, will accomplish what the lawsuits are not able to accomplish. May God bless your efforts to reach out and help those who share your world.

Part One
In the Beginning

1

Site History of Butterfly Ridge

The twenty-one-acre Butterfly Ridge property has been in the family since 1863. Originally the land was owned by Solomon Beery. Solomon's daughter, Mollie, married Jacob Bainter and gave birth to a son, Ira. Ira grew up, got married and had a daughter, Alice Sydney Bainter, my grandmother on my father's side. Alice received the land from her father and upon her passing, the land was transferred to my grandfather, Sheldon Kline.

While not a lot is known about the land use prior to Ira Bainter, it can be largely assumed that agriculture and logging were among the land's uses, as that was the primary way of making-a-living in the region at the time. We know that Ira Bainter used the acreage for agriculture. My dad has shared stories of harvesting a variety of produce from the property and going with his grandpa (Ira

Bainter) to the nearby towns of Logan and Nelsonville. Using his Ford Model A pick-up truck, my great-grandfather and my dad would sell the produce door-to-door and to small grocery stores. Watermelons, raspberries, and strawberries were among the crops that they sold out of the truck.

Corn and wheat were also grown on the site. My great-grandfather also raised livestock on the property including cows and horses. My grandmother raised rabbits on the site as well.

My great-grandfather was also well-known for his moonshine business. In fact, my father's first memory of his grandfather was visiting him in the Hocking County jail where he temporarily resided courtesy of a moonshine offense. My dad has shared that he thinks he knows where his grandfather hid the moonshine from the revenuers, but unfortunately dad's health prohibits him from taking me across the challenging, hilly landscape to look for the antique moonshine.

When Sheldon Kline, my grandfather, took control of the property he largely discontinued the agricultural use of the property. There is reason to believe that limited logging continued to take place on the property. Otherwise, the property was largely used for recreation with maintenance of the site being limited to annual mowing of existing fields. These fields comprised roughly two-thirds of the property.

Annual mowing of the property proved to be challenging due to the hilly nature of the site. In the early-1980's my grandfather quit mowing the section of the property which would later become known as the East Woods because of the steep terrain.

In the late 1980's the land was transferred from my grandfather to my father. My dad continued the maintenance regime with mowing the existing fields once or twice per year. However, in the late 90's my father quit mowing the field that paralleled the small stream on the site as well as a steep hillside adjacent to the field. This area would later become known as the Checkerboard. In the extreme south end of this former field, a one-tenth acre stand of Virginia pine took over. Over the ensuing twenty years, mixed hardwood tree species began to infiltrate the native pine stand.

The twenty-one-acre site was once a part of a much larger piece of property. The Bainter family holdings at one time extended a mile north to the intersection with Ohio Route 678 and included property on both sides of Ohio Route 374. Over time, the larger property was divided and sold. At the time that my father received the twenty-one acres, our property was bounded on two sides by extended family members. Changes in land ownership continued such that at the groundbreaking of Butterfly Ridge, the property was bounded on three sides by Crane Hollow Nature Preserve and only on a portion of the west side by extended family.

While a formal floristic survey of the site has never taken place, informal data has been kept since the early-90's. Plant diversity, especially in the fields that had been used agriculturally and had received annual mowing, was quite poor. Three species of plants largely dominated these fields; heath aster, goldenrod (early and Canada), and the dominant grass was broom sedge. All of these plants were indicators of poor soils.

Soil pH of the site tends toward acidic. And while formal soil testing has not been undertaken, the relative abundance of members of the Heath Family including deerberry and sourwood, along with plenty of Virginia pine, bear witness to the acidic nature of the soil. The soil of the site is a heavy clay, with occasional sandstone and a thin layer of shale rock.

The forested portion of the site is classic mixed hardwood forest. The common trees along the creek include white oak, ash, ironwood, and hazelnut. Many of the large ash trees along the creek have since succumbed to emerald ash borer. In the other forested sections of the site, tulip tree, red maple, and sassafras are the dominate tree species. Several species of oak, including red, scarlet, black, and chestnut oak occur throughout the site. In addition, on the south-facing slopes there is a sprinkling of Eastern hemlock, a tree which is much more common on north-facing slopes and within the deep hollows of the area.

On the northwest corner of the property, a small plantation, covering perhaps one-half acre, of Red Pine had been planted during the 1930's by the Civilian Conservation Corps. This plantation is still standing and thriving; however, hardwood trees have begun to work their way into the plantation. In the 1990's, Virginia pine was also added to this plantation.

In the west-central portion of the property a small wetland of perhaps one-quarter acre exists. This wetland is fed by runoff from the hillside to the east as well road runoff from Ohio Route 374. Standing water is normally present only following the spring thaw in April and May. This wetland eventually drains into the creek which serves as the headwaters for Snyder Creek, which drains into Crane Hollow and eventually to Pine Creek, Salt Creek, and the Scioto River. Bulrush, sensitive fern, and dear-tongue grass are the common plants in this small wetland.

As we began the development of Butterfly Ridge, we incorporated two pre-existing trails into the overall trail system. The trail that would eventually become known as the East Trail, was first created as a farm road by my great-grandfather so that he could access his farm fields with his Model A. This trail, which runs along the east property boundary we estimate to be roughly 100 years old.

In addition, the trail that would become known as the South Trail, was created in the early 1990's by my wife and I with our dog Pebbles. At the time, we created the route to provide a way to move from one field to another without having to fight through greenbrier. Pebbles the dog was a large mixed breed dog who loved to work. We would cut down small trees to clear the path, cut them into smaller pieces and then attach the pieces to Pebbles leash and let her drag it up the hill for us, which she thought was great fun.

Figure 1. Aerial photo of property circa 1995.

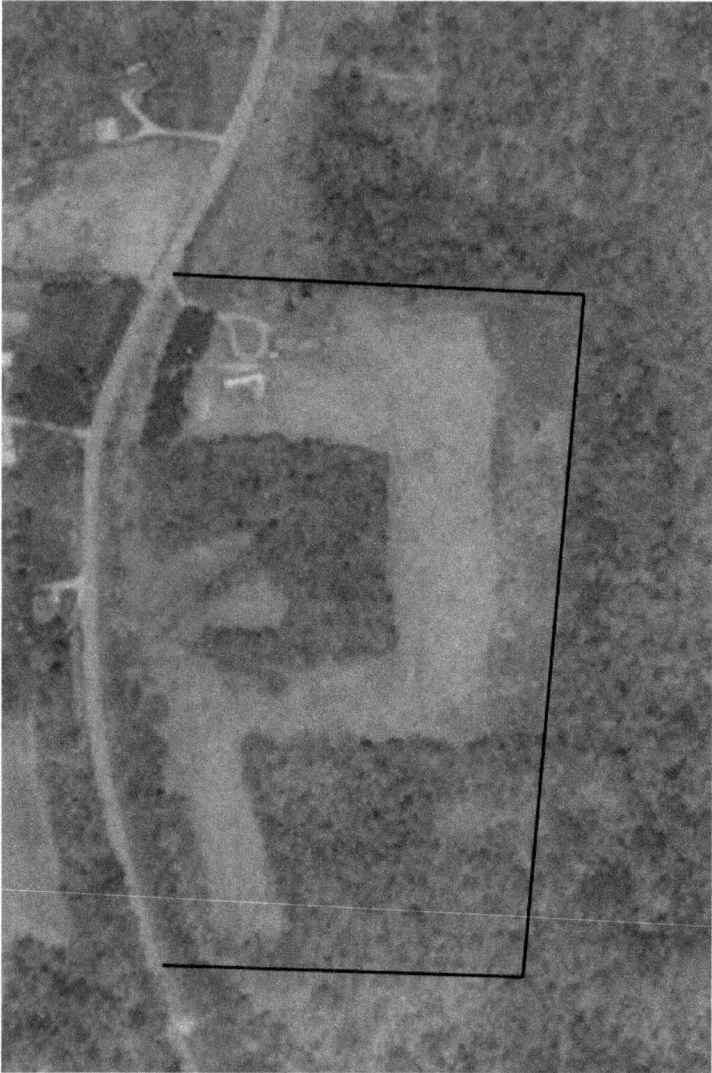

Figure 2. Aerial photo of property circa 2015.

2

Our Motivation

The idea of creating butterfly habitat on a large scale was conceived in early 2014. My dad had divided the twenty-one acres between my brother and I around 2010. I had received the south five acres, my brother the north five of the rectangle-shaped property. Dad had retained the eleven acres in the middle.

My family and I would go over to visit mom and dad for an hour or two on the weekends, but we would not really do anything with our five acres. We were not exploring very much, there was no snow sledding in the wintertime. Very independently of each other, both my wife and I began to feel guilty that we were not taking advantage of the property we had been blessed with.

The question turned to what could we do with five acres? We could have sold the timber on the property. Our five acres had the biggest trees of the original twenty-one acres, including quite large oaks. And while I am sure we could have made a small fortune selling the trees, this plan did not seem very fulfilling.

So, what did we know how to do that could utilize a piece of property? I didn't know how to farm on a large scale. Our area was already obscenely overloaded with rental cabins, plus we did not have the money to build cabins. What I knew how to do was . . . butterflies.

I had done monarch butterfly research in Arizona, starting the Southwest Monarch Study while being the education director at the Boyce Thompson Arboretum. As a part of my BTA duties, I had also led butterfly walks and moth lighting nights. I had also spent six years as the butterfly specialist at Franklin Park Conservatory in Columbus, Ohio. In that position I had cared for over a hundred species of tropical butterflies, researched their host plant requirements, led twice daily talks about butterflies, and taught butterfly gardening classes. Butterflies was what I knew how to do.

In addition, having engaged in so much butterfly-themed educational programming over the years, it had become very apparent that many people, including some who were bona fide nature nerds, had very little knowledge of the intricacies of the butterfly life cycle and their importance in the greater ecosystem. Not only were butterflies what I knew how to do, but there was also a significant need for the general public to have a better understanding of butterflies, as well as other pollinating insects.

So, we decided we would create a public garden dedicated to butterflies and their habitat on our five-acre piece of the property. My father approved of the idea which was very important. After all, if it worked out as we envisioned, there would be total strangers walking around through what had been his woods, plus we would have to use his driveway for visitors to access the site.

Another key factor in helping us to make the decision was our location near Hocking Hills State Park. One of the sites within the park, Old Man's Cave, received 3.5 million visitors per year. We thought if we could get one percent of those Old Man's Cave visitors to travel the four miles to our site, we would be in fine shape from the business perspective. In addition, with this knowledge of local tourism, our oldest daughter, Eileen, who was studying Business Management at Ohio University, helped us develop a business plan which also encouraged us to move forward.

However, in April 2014, a chain of events began which would completely alter our original plan for the project, which we had tentatively named Butterfly Ridge. In April, my wife's father passed away. John Purdy had been very successful in the construction business in Arizona and left a significant inheritance to his three children. This unexpected input of cash allowed us to think bigger in terms of facilities and infrastructure for the new project.

In October 2014, my mother passed away. A few weeks after mom's passing, my brother approached me about buying his north 5 acres. He offered us the family rate, the asking price probably barely covering the cost of the pole barn he had built on the site. With the unexpected cash from my father-in-law's passing, we were able to purchase the five acres from my brother.

In very early 2015, in a visit with my dad, he informed me that I needed to take him to a lawyer's office the following Monday. I inquired the purpose of the visit with the lawyer, hoping I had not messed-up something! With mom's passing he wanted to take mom's name off the deed for the remaining eleven acres and replace it with my name. However, the way he ultimately completed the transaction, he ended up giving me his eleven-acre piece which was wedged between the two five-acre pieces that I already owned. This restored the twenty-one acres back to essentially a single piece, now under my control.

My wife and I are people of faith and tend to believe that things happen for a reason. To us, the fact that all these different events played out in perfect order with virtually zero effort on our part could not be explained by coincidence or some sort of randomness. We absolutely believed that a higher power was laying out breadcrumbs for us to follow, and that we would be total cads if we did not follow the trail.

In the spring of 2015, we started in earnest with habitat and prep work. We cleared a woodland opening we had originally cleared in the middle 1990's. We also began removing trees from the locations of future parking lots and nature center. We also mowed the expected trail through the wetland and fields of the 21-acre site. The specifics of this work will be discussed in the Habitat chapters of this book.

In April 2015, with the expected trail locations roughed in, we began our monthly butterfly transects. It is important to note that the transects started very early in the habitat development process, so that 2015 could serve as a baseline year for our data collection. This baseline data would prove very important to confirm that our habitat work was actually working.

One thing that is important to note is that during this time I was still working as the "butterfly wrangler" at Franklin Park Conservatory. In addition, in July 2015 we moved from a rental property in Sugar Grove to the basement of my father's house. With the move, my commute of 40 miles one way increased to 51 miles one way. And while my official schedule at FPC was 30 hours per week, with the commute added in, I was spending over 50 hours per week either at FPC or in route to and from.

During the summer of 2015, we set a tentative opening date for Butterfly Ridge of July 1, 2017. As cold weather returned at the end of 2015, it became obvious that this opening date was in real jeopardy if I continued working at FPC five days per week. In April 2016 I quit my job at FPC so that I could focus my full attention to the Butterfly Ridge project.

Part Two
Habitats

3

Prairies

As mentioned previously, the plants growing in our ridgetop fields lacked diversity and were indicative of poor soils. We knew these plant species would not be conducive to our desires of increasing our local butterfly population. We were convinced that converting these abused fields to prairie was our ticket to increased butterfly activity.

The initial plan called for converting roughly 1.5 acres of field into prairie. Prior to any work on the ground we researched, seeking out the proper techniques to accomplish our goals. This research included internet searches of prairie conversion projects.

We also paid a visit to the Fairfield County Soil and Water office to meet with Dave Libben. While our site was in Hocking County, Dave was temporarily covering both Fairfield and Hocking counties. Dave shared suggestions for eliminating the current field so that we could start with a clean slate. The two options that would work on a large scale were chemical (Round-up) and mechanical.

I do think there is a time and place for Round-up herbicide and killing 1.5 acres of field is not that time and place. Spraying on such a large scale would have provided a strong potential for drift of the chemical, killing things that we did not want to kill. We were left with the mechanical option.

Dave also informed us that Soil and Water could help in other ways besides advise. They had equipment we could borrow. They could also provide what is known as an EQUIP grant. EQUIP stands for Environmental Quality Incentives Program and is a grant program to encourage landowners to conserve their land for wildlife and other conservation uses. This EQUIP grant could help us buy seed or other supplies for the prairie project.

Dave came and visited our site to offer suggestions. Many of his suggestions were common sense, such as reminding us to do the mechanical removal of the field with the elevational contours of the field, rather than against the contour, to limit erosion. He also noted that based on the abundance of broom sedge and goldenrod, he could safely predict that our soil pH was around 6.0, which was far too acidic for many prairie plants. He suggested we try to raise the pH to at least a 7.0. We would accomplish that by adding lime.

Work on the prairie began in the autumn of 2015. We decided to break the project into two years, with the first year being a smaller bite. Also leading to this decision was the fact that we were too late to apply for an EQUIP grant for 2016.

While my dad was never a large-scale farmer, he was a gardener, and dad's garden was about a quarter-acre in size. Over the years he had purchased a small Ford tractor with all the farming implements to try to make his garden prep easier. This would work to our advantage. Dad used his tractor and disc attachment in the autumn of 2015 to cut up the sod of two sections of the field; one section about one-quarter acre in size, the other a strip about ten feet wide and 100 feet long. We did this to make tilling in the spring of 2016 a little easier.

Also, in the autumn of 2015 I began to research plants that would be appropriate to plant in the prairie. All plant species that we would add to our prairie had to be native to Ohio. We wanted a good selection of butterfly nectar plants and caterpillar host plants. Much of the research for this information had already been done when I was researching for my book *Butterfly Gardening with Native Plants*.

We decided early on that we would use seed to populate the prairie, primarily in the name of cutting costs and maintaining flexibility. I did not want to be limited in my planting to what local garden centers had available, which in terms of native plants was virtually nothing. We acquired seeds from several sources. First of all, we had native milkweeds already on site, so I had gathered seed pods previously. We also purchased seed from

Roundstone Seed in Kentucky and Prairie Moon Nursery in Minnesota.

Over the winter we stratified the seed we had collected for the process. Stratification is the process by which you simulate winter in order to break dormancy within the seed. How we chose to accomplish this was to place the seed in a Ziploc bag with a damp paper towel. We labeled the outside of the bag with seed species, date we started the process, and date the process would be completed. We then placed the bag in the refrigerator. Most seed in the Midwest requires at least 60 days for this cold, damp treatment. Some seed, such as prairie grasses and bergamot, which were important components of our prairie project, did not require stratification.

One problem we discovered during this first winter was that the paper towel in the Ziploc bags had a tendency to mold. We began to check the bags periodically for mold. When mold was discovered, we removed the seed from the bag and paper towel and used a new bag and paper towel. When doing this, the day count did not need to start over.

We planned on growing the seed in our greenhouse. The greenhouse is a small hoop house (14' x 20') with a poly skin over a metal frame. In anticipation, we created a portable solar generator for the greenhouse. Using two 100W solar panels and two deep cycle marine batteries, we could have a self-charging infrastructure to run heat mats and lights so that we could start growing seeds while it was still cold outside. We acquired the plans for the solar generator from Jay Warmke of Blue Rock Station Living Center.

Inside the greenhouse we also deployed passive heating techniques. In the greenhouse we placed three 25-gallon black plastic trash cans filled with water. The idea is that during the daytime the sun would heat the water in the trash cans. That heat would then be released into the greenhouse at night. We also put an extra layer of plastic over the top of the greenhouse. At each end of the greenhouse, where the zippered doors were located, we stacked bales of hay at the base of the greenhouse to limit cold air entering the greenhouse at the bottom.

In mid-February 2016 we started our first batch of seeds. We used old seed flats we had collected. We placed newspaper in the bottom of the flats and then poured soil into the flats. We originally started with Miracle-Gro potting mix but switched after two seasons to Pro-Mix. We found that the Miracle-Gro product tended to produce a soil fungus which created an impenetrable layer at the soil surface, making water absorption by the soil (and plant) virtually impossible.

With the flats placed on the heat mat that was powered by the solar generator, we sprinkled seeds on top of the soil. The amount of soil we used to cover the seeds varied according to the size of the seed. Large seeds like milkweed received one-eighth to one-quarter inch of soil covering. Very small seeds, like bergamot and other mints, received no cover soil at all. We then placed empty flats upside down on top of the full flats and then placed another layer of plastic sheeting over the top of the flats, as yet another passive heating tool.

When April 2016 arrived, my dad began the tilling process in the sections of the field we had disced the previous autumn. Once the ground had thawed, we tilled the two areas every two weeks for a total of three tillings. Weather altered the schedule somewhat as dad refused to till mud for some crazy reason! The idea for the repeated tillings was to allow weed seeds in the soil to germinate and then go through with the tiller to chop them up. The more passes we could make with the tiller, the more of the existent seed bank we could successfully destroy.

After each tilling we applied lime to the two areas. For these first two sections we used bagged lime purchased from the local feed store. We applied a total of 1.5 tons of lime to these small sections combined. We spread the lime using a salt spreader dad had purchased previously to spread road salt on his driveway. The best recommendation I could find online regarding lime application suggest applying at a rate of four tons per acre to achieve an increase of 1.0 in pH.

After each section had been tilled three times, we used a roller filled with water and rolled one of the two sections. We wanted to see if compacting the soil prior to seeding would aid or diminish the success of the seed germination. We rolled both sections after spreading the seed to ensure better seed to soil contact. What we found over the next two years was that the pre-rolled section became much lusher, more quickly than the unrolled section.

Figure 3. Asa Kline rolling prairie after seeding.

The seed mix used in this initial planting was predominately prairie grass seed with leftover seed from our greenhouse planting tossed in. We seeded at a rate of eight pounds per acre. We used the same salt/lime spreader to spread the seed. The seed mix included Indian grass (*Sorghastrum nutans*), big bluestem (*Andropogon gerardi*), and side-oats grama (*Bouteloua curtipendula*).

Immediately after we seeded the areas, we flagged the locations of future trails through the prairie. After flagging the trails, and about a week after seeding the prairie grasses, we planted the plants we had started in the greenhouse in February. These plants were now 8-12 inches tall with well-developed root systems and could easily be transplanted. We enlisted the help of neighbors and church friends and easily planted 400 plants in a matter of a couple hours.

We planted a small orange flag with each plant. This way, if we experienced a prolonged drought after planting, we could easily find the plants again for watering purposes. We did have to water twice as the spring of 2016 was drier than normal.

At no point in 2016 did we mow these newly planted areas. I had people recommend that we mow, but I wanted to keep the process as natural as possible. The only section that we did mow was the trail that we had marked through the prairie.

In 2016 we were able to apply for an EQUIP grant for 2017. We were awarded a grant of a little over $700 for the 2017 growing season. We used most of that money to buy four tons of bulk lime to be used in the two new sections of prairie.

The 2017 prairie work was completed exactly the same as 2016 with one exception. Since the spring of 2017 was much wetter than 2016, we were only able to till the new sections twice, rather than three times, prior to planting. The two new sections were much larger in size, encompassing a little over a half-acre each.

Figure 4. Locations of prairie plantings at Butterfly Ridge.

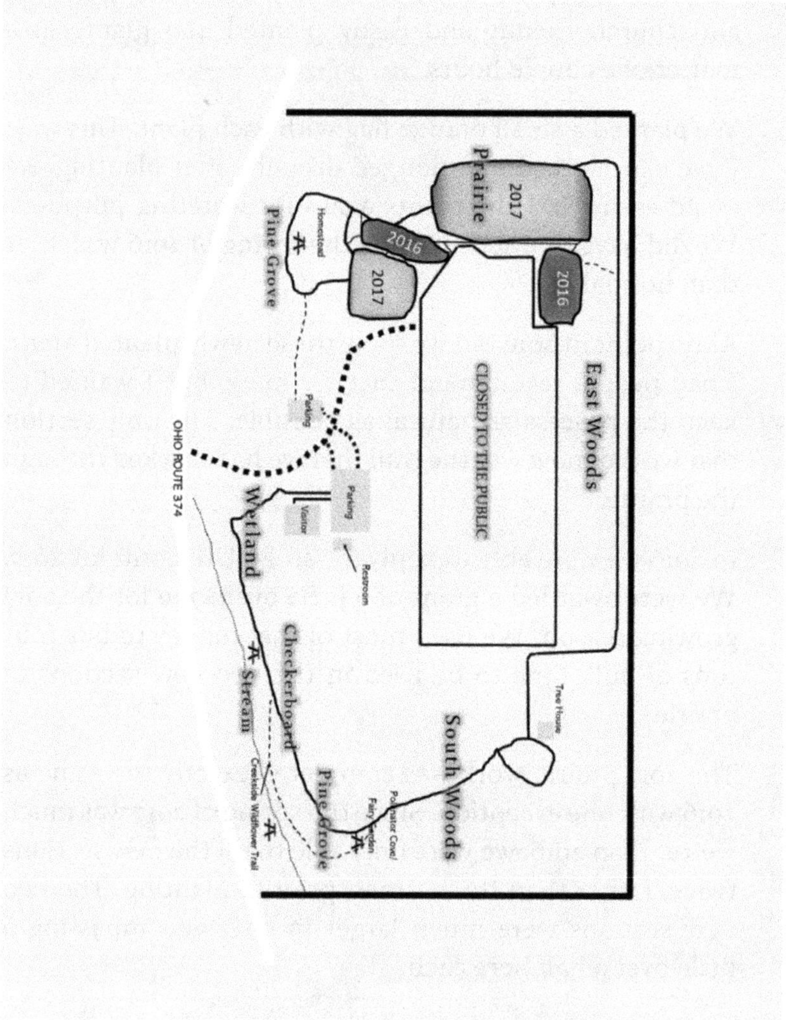

The same general seed mix was used with one exception, that being the addition of little bluestem (Schizachyrium scoparium) to the mix. In the two new sections of prairie we planted nearly 1,500 plants that we had grown in the greenhouses. Yes, in the off-season we added a second greenhouse with a second portable solar generator. Supplemental watering was not necessary for the 2017 prairie.

One of the differences we noticed very quickly was the increased abundance of weeds in the new sections of prairie. We think that is directly attributable to the missed third tilling. On a weekly basis during the summer we hand-pulled foxtail grass out of the new sections of prairie. Foxtail can easily take over a site if permitted, so diligence was required to prevent this invasive weed from taking hold.

Another plant that we sought out for destruction was horse nettle (*Solanum carolinense*). While this plant is a native, it is a colonizer of disturbed ground that can temporarily take over a site. It is also beset with significant and painful spines. The final nail in the coffin so to speak was that there is only a single moth that uses it as a caterpillar host plant (Carolina Sphinx) and that primarily only bumble bees visit the flowers. It seemed like a plant that had very limited positives and significant negatives.

Table 1. Plant species initially planted in prairie.

Scientific name	Common Name	N-nectar h-host
Andropogon gerardi	Big Bluestem	h-Satyrs, Skippers, Common Wood Nymph
Ascelepias hirtella	Green Milkweed	h-Monarch
Asclepias syriaca	Common Milkweed	N h-Monarch
Asclepias tuberosa	Butterfly Weed	N h-Monarch
Asclepias verticillata	Whorled Milkweed	N h-Monarch
Aster azureus	Sky Blue Aster	N h-Pearl Crescent
Aster novae-anglinae	New England Aster	N h-Pearl Crescent
Blephilia ciliata	Downy Wood Mint	N
Bouteloua curtipendula	Side-oats Grama	h-Satyrs, Skippers, Common Wood Nymph
Cacalia plantaginifolium	Indian Plantain	N
Cirsium altissimum	Tall Thistle	N
Cirsium discolor	Field Thistle	N
Eryngium yuccifolium	Rattlesnake Master	N
Eupatorium coelestinum	Mistflower	N

Helianthus tuberosus	Jerusalem Artichoke	N
Lespedeza capitata	Roundhead Bush Clover	H-Cloudywings and Hoary Edge
Lespedeza violacea	Violet Bush Clover	H-Cloudywings and Hoary Edge
Liatris spicata	Blazing Star	N
Liatris squarrosa	Colic Root	N
Monarda fistulosa	Bergamot	N
Pycnanthemum tenuifolium	Mountain Mint	N
Ratibida columnaris	Mexican Hat	N
Satureja vulgaris	Wild Basil	N
Schizachyrium scoparium	Little Bluestem	h-Satyrs, Skippers, Common Wood Nymph
Senna hebecarpa	American Senna	h-Sulphurs
Silphium perfoliatum	Cup Plant	N
Silphium terebinthinaceum	Prairie Dock	N
Sorghastrum nutans	Indian Grass	h-Satyrs, Skippers, Common Wood Nymph
Tridens flavus	Purpletop	h-Satyrs, Skippers, Common Wood Nymph
Verbesina alternifolia	Wingstem	N h-Silvery Checkerspot

Another maintenance issue that developed within all of the prairie areas was the infiltration of woody plants. Many people mow to take down the woodies. The problem with mowing however, at least in terms of woodies, is that the mowing does not eliminate the woody plants, it just prunes them. The woodies will continue to send up stump sprouts forcing you to continue mowing. Our approach to the woody plants was to dig them up by the roots, or at least cut them off at the roots.

I am not a big fan of mowing. Mowing should have some end game beyond neatness, but unfortunately that is one of the few things that mowing accomplishes. No mowing, beyond keeping trails cleared, has happened in our prairie nor will happen in our prairie. For many folks this is very hard to understand, because as a culture we have embraced mowing and neatness in our landscapes for generations.

Among the pitfalls of mowing is the wanton destruction of the very pollinators that we are trying to protect. Grass skipper caterpillars for example overwinter within the stems of prairie grasses. When warm weather arrives in the spring and the grasses begin to green up, these caterpillars will migrate down to the base of the plant to feed on the new growth. Mowing our prairies anytime between September and April will destroy the next season's grass skippers.

In fact, many of the butterflies that we associate with prairies, grasslands, and fields, including grass skippers, satyrs, common wood nymph, and pearl crescent all spend the winter as caterpillars in those same fields. Mowing when these organisms are in this vulnerable phase makes no sense.

Our plan for large scale maintenance of the prairies is to take a more natural approach which will focus largely on burning. The current plan will be to burn the three largest sections of prairie every three years on a rotating basis. Rotating the sections that are burned each year will reduce the negative aspects of burning; largely the destruction of caterpillars and chrysalises that may be overwintering in the prairie. We may decide that the prairie does not need to be burned this often to eliminate woody and invasive species and therefore reduce the number butterflies killed in the burning process.

Generally speaking, we are very pleased with how the prairie plantings have developed and matured. However, there is one thing we would definitely change given the opportunity to start completely over. The change we would make would be to use a much smaller percentage of tall grass species in the seed mix and a much higher percentage of short grasses.

When we seeded the grasses for the prairie, the mix we created was roughly 75 percent tall grass versus 25 percent short grass. In hindsight, I think we should have flipped those numbers around and seeded more heavily with the short grass species.

Early in the season, through late July or so, the height of the native perennials in the prairie matches or are slightly taller than the grasses, making it easy for butterflies and other pollinators to find and utilize those wildflowers. However, with the month of August, the tall grasses experience a growth spurt as they prepare for inflorescence production. What this means is that in late summer the grasses are considerably taller than the native perennial wildflowers, making it more difficult for butterflies to utilize those flowers. A stronger emphasis on shorter grasses would have improved the visibility and availability of the wildflowers throughout the season.

In response to this, our plan moving forward will be to convert smaller tracts, on the order of 1000 square feet at a time, to short grass/wildflower plots within the tall grass prairie. Currently the plan to accomplish this will be to till these small tracts repeatedly in the spring, plant late May, and then harvest the seed of the tall grasses adjacent to the short grass plots before they have a chance to seed into the new tracts. The harvested seed will be used as a part of our seed giveaway program which we offer to help others develop more butterfly friendly landscapes.

Figure 5. Northern-most prairie planting after two years.

4

Woodland Openings

Our first habitat project, once we decided to create Butterfly Ridge, was to re-open a clearing in the forest. This area in the South Woods was near the black oak that would eventually be home to the Treehouse. This particular quarter-acre site had been originally cleared in the 1990's as my parents had plans to build their house here. Over time my mom changed her mind and decided the house would be built in one of the fields.

As my wife and I considered where to begin habitat work, this old clearing came to mind immediately. While trees had moved back into the clearing, they were tall and thin, making them easy cut with the chain saw. The tree species composition of this area which would become known as the Clearing was largely winged sumac, black locust, red maple, and sourwood.

Figure 6. The Clearing indicated by white circle.

In 6-8 weeks, my son and I had re-opened the original clearing. However, we had a desire to expand the Clearing to an extent which required cutting down some larger trees. One challenge we faced was that many of these larger trees were tied together by grape vines in the tree canopy. As we cut one particularly large black locust, a grape vine stopped the tree in mid-fall, pulling the tree backwards where it got hung-up in a large red maple. Eventually, we had to tie a heavy rope to the black locust and pull the tree into the Clearing using our pick-up truck.

With the trees removed, the understory was able to develop. The plant species which gained a foothold included Japanese honeysuckle, white snakeroot, downy lobelia, bead grass, and purpletop grass. We also planted bergamot, butterflyweed, downy wood mint, mistflower, and asters within this clearing.

Another challenge which we faced, specifically in planting this area, was damage from wildlife. Deer, we assume, ate the bergamot, which surprised us in that deer, nor any other wildlife that we are aware of, normally eat plants in the mint family. In addition, some animal, we are not sure who, continually dug up one specific aster plant. We replanted the aster two more times in the same hole. Eventually we had to surround the plant with bricks to keep it from being dug up yet again.

Our maintenance plan for this space is different than any of the other spaces at Butterfly Ridge. In this clearing we selectively allow certain tree species to return to the clearing. The favored tree species include all oaks, black locust, and sweet birch. The reason oaks receive preferential treatment is because it is the caterpillar host plant of the banded hairstreak, a small butterfly which we exclusively find in the

Figure 7. Banded Hairstreak in the Clearing.

clearing. Black locust is preferred because of being the caterpillar host plant for the silver spotted skipper.

The preferential treatment for sweet birch is a little more complicated. Sweet birch is not a host for any butterfly species; however, it does host wooly aphids. Wooly aphids are food for the harvester butterfly caterpillar, the only carnivorous butterfly in North America. Therefore, favoring sweet birch indirectly favors the harvester.

Figure 8. Silver-spotted Skipper.

Figure 9. Harvester.

With oak and black locust, we allow the trees to achieve a height of 8-10 feet at which point we cut the tree at the base. We do this to encourage stump sprouting, as hairstreak females tend to lay eggs on shorter oak trees rather than taller. In addition, hairstreak caterpillars will pupate beneath the leaf litter on the ground. Smaller trees better ensure that the caterpillars will safely find the leaf litter. Regarding the sweet birch, we do not control its height in an attempt to maximize new growth available to the aphids.

On the south edge of the Clearing we also transplanted nearly one hundred violets from the northeast corner of the property in the area known as the East Woods. Violets are the caterpillar host plant for the fritillary butterflies. However, fritillaries do not normally fly deep into the forest looking for violets. Therefore, we moved the violets to a location where the fritillaries would be more apt to find them. In addition, the fritillaries overwinter in the caterpillar stage of the life cycle. The small caterpillar will climb large trees in search of deep cracks in the bark in which to wedge themselves for the winter. For this reason, we transplanted the violets to the wooded edge so that access to large trees would be facilitated for the caterpillars.

As mentioned, when discussing the history of the Butterfly Ridge site, the area that was later to become Checkerboard was once a field, maintained through agriculture and annual mowing. My father quit mowing this area in the 1990's, allowing a mixed hardwood forest and Virginia pine to come up in its place.

Figure 10. Sweet White Violet in Clearing.

Our original intent was to re-open this field, and plant and maintain it much like the prairie. We invited some family and friends over to start the project. We had three chain saws running for an entire weekend and barely got a quarter-acre cleared. At that rate, we were afraid it would take multiple lifetimes to finish the task, so we thought again about the plan.

In forestry school at Northern Arizona University, I had learned the value of edge effect to wildlife. I also knew that some butterflies preferred woodland openings. We therefore changed our approach. Rather than clearing the entire three-acre field, we would cut small chunks out of the field. We would cut these openings in a checkerboard appearance, to allow for maximum edge effect. In fact, by cutting in this pattern, we approximately doubled the available edge effect.

Figure 11. Brandon Kremer removing trees in the Checkerboard.

Figure 11. Brandon Kremer removing trees in the Checkerboard.

To date we have cut five of these openings in the old field and anticipate at least three more.

One challenge in managing the Checkerboard is in maintaining the openings. While in the original clearing we have allowed certain trees to move back into the space, the Checkerboard openings will be kept free of trees. We have used primarily mechanical methods (digging) to remove any new trees that do try to enter the openings. We are fearful that trying to use burning to keep these areas "clean" could have potentially bad results due to the proximity of the forest. If we are unable to keep up mechanically, we may need to resort to using herbicide or time sensitive mowing.

5

Wetland

The Butterfly Ridge wetland is in the middle of the property, adjacent to State Route 374 and is fed largely by run-off from the highway and a very small drainage that originates across the highway. The wetland drains into Snyder Hollow, which eventually empties into Crane Hollow and ultimately into the Scioto River.

The wetland has slow-moving surface water from the spring thaw until late May or early June. In especially wet years, this surface water may continue into July. In most years, there is no surface water in the autumn and therefore historically this area was mowed annually at this time.

While surface water may disappear in the middle of summer, subsurface water continues to move throughout the summer. This subsurface water is frequently just a few inches below the soil surface.

Figure 12. Location of Wetland at Butterfly Ridge.

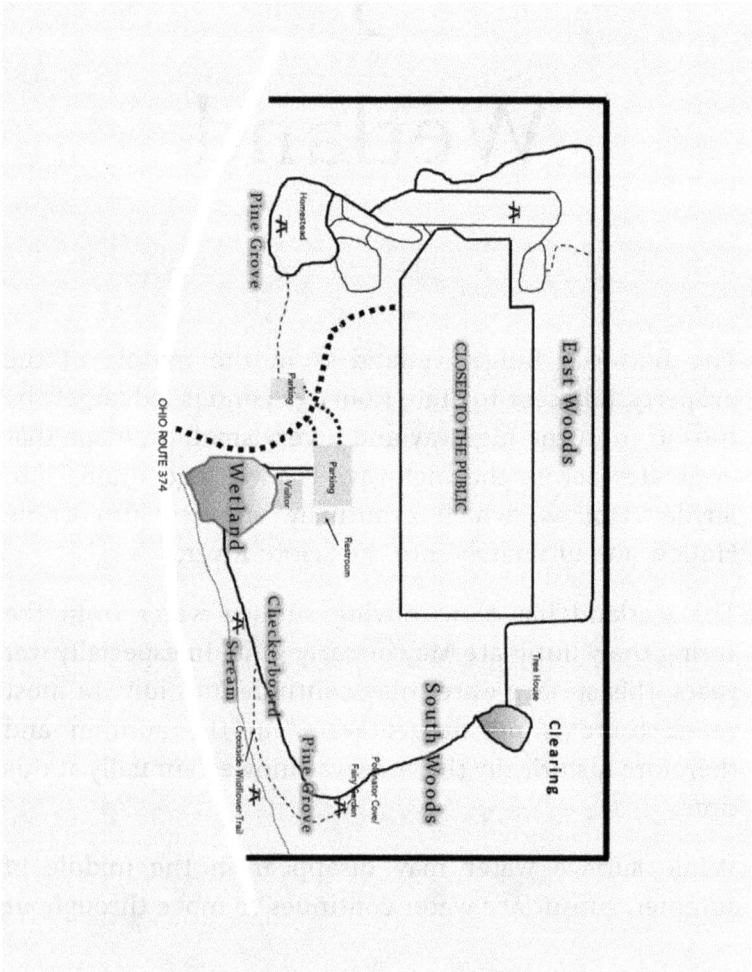

In 2015, as we were beginning work on Butterfly Ridge, the flora of the wetland consisted largely of bulrush, sensitive fern, and cut grass. In elevated areas adjacent to the wetland, ironweed and wingstem thrived. Unfortunately, invasive Canada thistle was also prevalent in the wetland area.

We found the wetland somewhat disappointing in its early condition, however. While the floral display in late August and September was quite impressive, the rest of the growing season was . . . meh.

We contacted Lynn Holtzman, a hydrologist and instructor at Hocking College. Lynn visited our site and we presented to him our dilemma of poor blooming in the wetland. We had a list of things we wanted to plant, but we were unsure whether there were adequate water resources to keep new wetland plants hydrated.

Lynn used his soil probe to check for subsurface water and found a plentiful subsurface flow three inches deep. And this was July! He confirmed that our planting plans could proceed.

We had already started buttonbush in the greenhouse a few years prior, so we quickly planted those. Lynn had warned us regarding buttonbush that it could potentially take over the site. This did not especially concern us; buttonbush was native and an excellent butterfly nectar plant that bloomed in early summer. Plus, we could always dig it up if it got out of control.

We also developed our list of seed to acquire as soon as possible so we could continue planting in 2018. Top priority on the seed list included swamp milkweed, turtlehead, swamp aster, cup plant, and cardinal flower.

We were able to secure local seed sources for these species. However, the turtlehead seed did not germinate, forcing us to purchase plants instead. These plants we acquired from Scioto Gardens Nursery, an outstanding native plant nursery in Delaware, Ohio. While the turtlehead is not a nectar source for butterflies, it is a host plant for the Baltimore checkerspot butterfly. And while we had never observed this butterfly species on the property, or even nearby, we wanted the host plant to be available if a female checkerspot dropped in.

In addition to using seed as a source for plants, we also took advantage of cuttings. Another plant species we wanted to add to the wetland was willow, as red-spotted purple and viceroy use willow as a host. Rather than purchasing willow trees or trying to capture the windblown seed, we took cuttings of native willow (sandbar willow) growing a few miles away along Pine Creek. The willow cuttings were cared for in the greenhouse and within a year we had 24-inch-tall willow whips.

In 2019, the planting work of 2018 paid off with the bloom of large masses of cup plant. During the August transect of 2019 over eighty swallowtails were counted, with most of them found amongst the cup plant. Strategic placement of swamp milkweed and swamp aster also paid, not only as nectar sources, but several monarch caterpillars were collected from the milkweed. The buttonbush also provided a wealth of nectar opportunities for butterflies visiting the Wetland.

Figure 13. Tiger Swallowtail nectaring on cup plant.

Figure 14. Butterflies nectaring on buttonbush.

6

Microhabitats

While much of the work we did in preparing Butterfly Ridge was on a large scale, there were also some very important projects that were on a much smaller scale. These smaller projects were tackled to meet a specific need or to take advantage of a unique habitat opportunity.

Outhouse

Since Butterfly Ridge would only be open six months of the year, we applied to the state of Ohio to receive a waiver from the rules that normally apply to public restrooms. Following the rules would had made the restrooms extremely costly and quite possibly would have prevented Butterfly Ridge from becoming reality.

In place of restrooms with running water and flush toilets, we installed an outhouse with a 1000-gallon concrete vault that would set under the outhouse. Considering that this project was taking place in Hocking County, Ohio, where flat land does not exist, the outhouse ended-up resting on the side of a hill.

A problem that we quickly noticed with the placement of the outhouse was that the two uphill sides of the outhouse tended to collect water at the base of the structure. We recognized this as a wetland opportunity, albeit a very small one. The area in question was approximately 12 inches wide and 24 feet long.

The outhouse sat in the shade for most of the day, so we needed plants that would tolerate both wet conditions and shade. In response we planted false nettle around the base of the outhouse. False nettle prefers extra moisture and will tolerate a variety of sun conditions. Plus, false nettle is the caterpillar host plant for red admiral, question mark, and eastern comma butterflies.

Figure 15. False nettle planted at base of outhouse.

The false nettle has done great in this location and we have observed several red admiral caterpillars taking advantage of the new plantings.

The Ditch

The Ditch is the space between the Butterfly Ridge nature center and the parking lot. At this point, perhaps it would be appropriate to describe in greater detail the lay of the land around the nature center.

The nature center is located on the side of a hill. When we chose this site for the facility, we wanted a location close to the highway where potential visitors would be able to see it. However, our wetland is directly adjacent to the highway and we did not want to disrupt this delicate habitat in any way. With this in mind, we built the nature center slightly uphill from the wetland.

Unfortunately, the site we selected still had an issue; the hillside drained directly through where we wanted the center. To avoid issues with flooding, we built the nature center on stilts, so that water would run under the building.

As we thought about this, we still had a few concerns. What if we wanted to do any sort of addition in front of the building, such as a stage? We would still have a water problem. Also, we placed the guts (batteries, inverters, etc.) of our solar power system under the building. Would we have flooding issues with that equipment?

Rather than continuing to see the natural drainage of the hillside as a problem, we looked upon this excess water as an opportunity to create additional wetland habitat. We asked our excavator to dig a small trench between the parking lot and the nature center. Therefore, any water that ran off the parking lot would run into the new trench and be channeled into the seasonal stream that ran slightly north of the nature center.

Figure 16. The Ditch between parking lot and nature center.

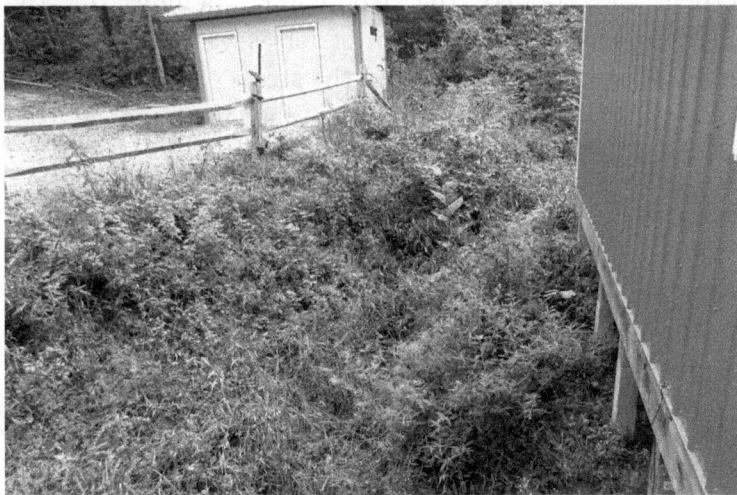

This trench, much like the area around the outhouse, created opportunity to plant water-loving nectar and host plants for butterflies. Since the creation of The Ditch, we have added cup plant, buttonbush, cardinal flower, glade mallow, aster, and bergamot. In the early and midsummer, The Ditch is quite a butterfly hotspot that was created by looking upon a problem as an opportunity.

Brush Piles

In Ohio, we have a few butterfly species who overwinter as adult butterflies including eastern comma, question mark, and mourning cloak. How do these butterflies accomplish such a feat? They spend the winter hidden in brush and rock piles or they hide behind loose bark on dying and dead trees.

When we created the woodland openings in the checkerboard, a large amount of debris was created. As we cut down trees, we bucked up the stems of the trees to be used as future firewood. Branches that were removed from the trees were piled and left in the openings.

Some of these piles, closest to the trail, were chipped and used as mulch on the trails. Piles farther off the trail remained in place, to be used by overwintering butterflies. By hiding in the piles, the butterflies are insulated to a degree from the cold and snow of winter.

Overwintering butterflies also take advantage of antifreeze-like chemicals which prevent ice crystals from forming within their bodies. Butterflies can withstand colder temperatures than what seems logical. The key to this is staying dry. If they have protection from moisture, they can survive very cold winter temperatures.

Figure 17. Brush piles in the Checkerboard.

7

Invasive Species

As we began to develop Butterfly Ridge, the question of how to manage invasive plant species was one of our first issues we had to address. With some of the invasive plant species, admitting defeat and moving on was the only viable option. Japanese honeysuckle (*Lonicera japonica*) fell into this category.

Japanese honeysuckle is a vining plant with white flowers, blooming primarily in late spring but with occasional blooms throughout the summer. On our property, not only was this honeysuckle a common groundcover, but it also climbs into trees and onto fences. Ours seemed to spread by runners that would root at the leaf nodes.

We estimated that the honeysuckle covered nearly forty percent of the property. Simply thinking about how to control the plant was exhausting, let alone trying to implement a strategy. Our strategy was simple; try to keep it out of newly created areas. With this in mind, we removed honeysuckle from the developing prairies and did not waste time trying to remove well-established clumps from elsewhere.

Figure 18. Tiger Swallowtail on Japanese honeysuckle.

Another invasive species that we decided to not aggressively remove is Canada thistle (Cirsium arvense). This thistle grows primarily in the Wetland and while it is present, its current influence over the site is minimal. Our concern in trying to remove this thistle was the collateral damage to other plants that we wanted to retain. In addition, the fact that the seed of this plant stays in the seed bank for so long made physical removal a multi-year, extremely disruptive process. Instead, we will attempt to limit additional seed drop from this species by routine deadheading.

With other invasive species we have taken a much more aggressive approach. Perhaps our most aggressive measures have been implemented on privet. I am unsure which privet we have, whether it is the European or the Chinese or some other one. They are all listed as invasive in our county.

Privet is a woody plant, growing to the size of a large shrub in favorable habitat. At Butterfly Ridge, the privet is most prevalent in the Wetland, but is present elsewhere as well. It spreads largely due to birds eating the fruits and dispersing the seeds. Smaller plants, to eighteen inches tall, can simply be pulled up by hand as the root systems are fairly sparse.

Large specimens of privet need to be cut down with chain saws. At Butterfly Ridge, we have cut down plants with stems as much as eighteen inches wide at the soil surface. Privet is notorious for sending up root suckers and stump sprouts after it has been cut. These we spray with herbicide to keep controlled.

Another invasive that we will be taking a much more aggressive approach with is miscanthus grass, sometimes known as silvergrass. Silvergrass was introduced to Butterfly Ridge in the late 1990's by my dad. He had received four plants from his aunt. Dad planted these four plants along the driveway near the house.

Figure 19. Great Spangled Fritillary on privet.

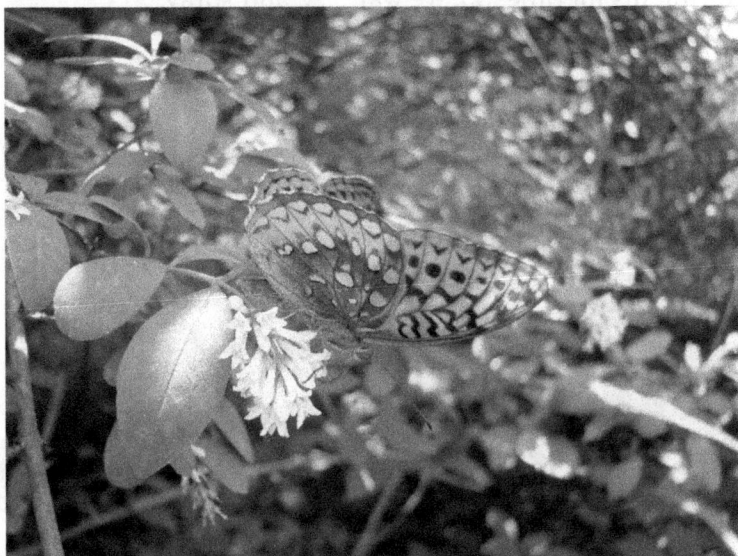

We now have large thickets of silvergrass in the orchard, next to both chicken houses, on the bank next to the house and driveway, on the bank next to the highway (nearly a quarter-mile from the original planting), in the Clearing, and in the fields.

Our initial response to the silvergrass was to dig it up, which was highly effective for those particular clumps. However, we have found in the last two years that the grass seeds and spreads far faster than we can dig it up. With this in mind, for the 2020 growing season we will be applying herbicide to kill the escaping silvergrass.

Sadly, this will not immediately stop the incursion. My dad has made it very clear that the original four plants that he received from his aunt are not to be touched; at least not during his lifetime. So, we wait . . . and spray.

Figure 20. Miscanthus grass.

Another highly invasive grass that is being battled is Japanese stilt grass. It spread onto the site in the early 2010's. We have been using a similar approach as that of the silvergrass; pulling it up and destroying it. Once it gets a little size on it, it pulls up quite easily, but it is back-breaking work. And much like the silvergrass, our efforts are simply not keeping pace with the spread of the grass. In 2020, we will also employ herbicide to keep this invasive under control.

We have other invasive species that we manage as well. Multiflora rose, Japanese barberry, autumn olive, and tree of heaven are all routinely dug on the site. We then monitor for root and stump sprouts and spray with herbicide accordingly.

Using herbicide is not our preferred method for dealing with invasive species for a variety of reasons. First of all are the potential health impacts to the person doing the spraying. For this reason, as the director of Butterfly Ridge, I am the only person who sprays. I do not want to risk the health of our interns with these products.

Another reason we are reluctant to spray herbicide is the threat of drift and collateral damage. Our invasive plants are of course growing up through and among desirable plants. Collateral damage to beneficial plants weighs heavily on our thinking.

However, the invasiveness of these plants, and the lack of effective alternative methods of control, leave us no choice. It is use herbicide or be taken over.

Which brings me to my next point. To my knowledge, of the nine invasive species that we battle daily in our effort to promote butterfly conservation, only one of them was intentionally planted on the site. And despite the renowned reputation for invasiveness that these plant species have, many of them are readily available in the nursery trade.

In a quick internet search, I found what Better Homes and Gardens had to say about Miscanthus grass, "Miscanthus, a prized ornamental grass, is a garden specimen with a graceful, vase-like shape that fills the garden with soft, airy forms. Also known as maiden grass, miscanthus looks good even when it's not in bloom. When it does bloom, the fine foliage is topped by silvery seed heads. The plants can grow quite large; look for dwarf varieties for smaller gardens."

There was absolutely no mention of the invasive tendency of this plant. I quickly found that I could order Japanese honeysuckle on Amazon and that Home Depot sold Japanese barberry. Through Etsy I could purchase multiflora rose and tree of heaven.

And finally, Southern Living had this to say about privet, "Although one species makes a fine landscape tree, privets are first and foremost hedge plants. They take well to shearing and can be clipped into almost any shape. In spring or early summer, all bear abundant clusters of showy, white to creamy white flowers that are highly fragrant. Some people don't care for the cloyingly sweet scent and the pollen may cause allergic reactions. Bees and wasps also swarm to the flowers. Clipped hedges produce fewer flowers, as shearing removes most of the flower buds. Blossoms are followed by small, berrylike, blue-black fruit. Birds eat them and distribute the seeds everywhere with the result that seedlings come up everywhere, too. Since most privets will grow well in any kind of soil, vigilance is required to keep them from taking over. Most make good container subjects. They are resistant to browsing deer."

At least Southern Living magazine acknowledged that privet seeds germinate readily. Unfortunately, they did not go all the way to discouraging the plant's use in the home landscape. And if you go to Amazon, you can purchase multiple privet species, several with free shipping!

The lack of responsibility being shown by garden centers and other retailers is appalling. And, because of people like them, selling plants like these, people like me will continue having to battle to create butterfly-friendly habitat like this.

8

Role of

Butterfly Bush

We have planted butterfly bush near our nature center, with less than stellar results. However, butterfly bush has been a hot button topic of late in reference to its invasive tendencies. Some folks have been arguing that at no point should butterfly bush be planted and that pre-existing butterfly bushes should be removed, all on the grounds of invasiveness.

There have been three basic arguments to support this opinion. First, because butterfly bush is not native to the United States (it is native to China) and has become invasive in certain parts of America, it should not be planted anywhere. There is some value to this argument. Yes, in certain states butterfly bush has become a noxious weed, taking over large areas of natural habitat. Ohio is one of the states, while not receiving noxious status, where butterfly bush is considered invasive. With that said however, I have grown butterfly bush in southeast Ohio for eight years and not once have I found a seedling or a root clone. In fact, my butterfly bush has had a terrible time surviving the winter. My hunch is that the escape of butterfly bush, at least in Ohio, has more to do with landscaping/gardening technique than with the butterfly bush itself.

At Butterfly Ridge, we have planted butterfly bush adjacent to the nature center. As I grow butterfly bush, I do not water it, fertilize it, or mulch it. In my yard every plant is very much on its own. One thing I do practice religiously is deadheading of spent flowers. If spent flowers are removed, then seedlings cannot start.

Figure 21. Painted Lady nectaring on butterfly bush.

Secondly, in the US there are no butterflies or moths who use butterfly bush as a caterpillar host plant and therefore by planting it you are preventing reproduction of our lepidopteran friends. This also has a certain amount of merit. However, I have yet to find anyone who plants their entire home landscape in a monoculture of butterfly bush. Likewise, this same argument could be used for marigolds, begonias, petunias, daylilies, hostas, and a wide range of other non-native plants, of which I have seen entire yards planted in, and of which there are 'societies' to encourage the planting of these evils.

Finally, there are claims that butterfly bush flower nectar is inferior to native flower nectar. I decided to research into this. I could not find any specific research that declared butterfly bush nectar to be bad or lacking in nutrition. I did find a research paper by Gao Chen, et al (2014) in which butterfly bush sugar content was measured. Chen, using butterfly bush plants in their native China, found that sugar concentration ranged from 17-33 percent, with an average of 24 percent.

In another paper by Hill and Pierce (1989), the authors, using Imperial Hairstreak in Australia, fed butterflies a diet of 0, 1, 25, and 50 percent sugar content and then tested the butterfly's longevity and fecundity against the diet the butterflies consumed. What Hill and Pierce found was that the butterflies on the 25 percent sugar content diet had the greatest longevity of all diets. Also, fecundity (essentially the number of eggs produced) was positively impacted by the two higher sugar concentrations. However, butterflies on the 50 percent sugar content diet tended to become obese which actually cost them longevity.

In addition, Hill and Pierce also tinkered with the protein content of the butterfly's diet. What the authors found was that nectar protein levels had no effect on longevity or fecundity.

When I put these two studies together, I am led to believe that the 24 percent sugar content of butterfly bush nectar should not be a problem. If the nectar was not sufficient, then butterflies would not consume it. What we have found at Butterfly Ridge the last two years, is that butterflies have largely ignored the butterfly bush in favor of native cup plant and ironweed.

Another argument that I have heard others use is that butterfly bush nectar is higher in sucrose than in glucose or fructose and therefore has an addictiveness about it. In Culin (1995), the author does document that butterfly bush does have an unusually high concentration of sucrose in its sugar composition. But to say that butterfly bush nectar has an addictive quality is silly, since I have observed countless butterflies turn their noses up at butterfly bush in favor of bergamot, cup plant, and ironweed. What drug addict would decline a hit of his favorite drug for a sprig of broccoli?!

Don't get me wrong, as I have shared throughout this writing, at Butterfly Ridge we have been all about using native plants to attract butterflies. However, shaming people into ripping out the butterfly bush at the corner of their residential lot is a human control tactic and nothing else. A single butterfly bush in your yard is not the end of anybody's world. Coupled with dedicated deadheading and an ample supply of native nectar and host plants, butterfly bush can provide a nice accent in places where butterfly bush is not on a noxious weed list.

This article first appeared in the Bloggerfly blog of the Butterfly Ridge Butterfly Conservation Center website.

Chen Gao, et al. 2014. Inflorescence scent, color, and nectar properties of "butterfly bush" (Buddleja davidii) in its native range. Flora 209 (2014) 172-178.

Culin Joseph. 1995. Relationship of Butterfly Visitation with Nectar Qualities and Flower Color in Butterfly Bush, Buddleia Davidii. News of the Lepidopterist Society, 1997.

Hill C.J. and N.E. Pierce. 1989. The effect of adult diet on the biology of butterflies. Oecologia (1989) 81:249-257

Part Three

Is It Working?

9

Data

Early in the history of Butterfly Ridge we began gathering data on the butterflies that called our site home. The initial transects began in April 2015, before any significant habitat work had begun. I knew that if we were successful in growing our local butterflies, we would need the science to back it up.

Transects were conducted during the first week of each month, from April through October. The date of the transect varied based on weather. Typically, on the first of each month we checked the seven-day weather forecast and picked the date that had the most favorable weather forecast that also worked with my off-site work schedule. Keep in mind, during the first year of the transect I was also working away from Butterfly Ridge.

In the early months of the year, April and May, weather can be quite unpredictable and unfriendly to butterfly activity for multiple days at a time. If a suitable transect date could not be found during the first week of the month, the earliest acceptable date was chosen within the first ten days of the month.

The transect route initially included: a roughed in loop trail through the Checkerboard, the wooded section of trail that connected the Checkerboard to the Clearing, the loop around the Clearing, the trail through the three eastern most sections of the Prairie, and the loop trail around the Homestead. In 2017, the loop through the western most section of prairie, adjacent to the Homestead Loop, was added to the Prairie section of the transect. Also in 2017, the trail through the Wetland was added to the transect. The Wetland section of the transect begins at the Ditch on the east side of the nature center and continues down the trail to the boundary with the Checkerboard. In addition, in 2017 the rough loop trail through the Checkerboard was abandoned and replaced with the current direct trail through the section.

On these transects, our intent was to identify and tally every butterfly we observed within fifteen feet of the trail. For unknown butterflies, a photo was taken, with the photo number recorded on the datasheet for future identification. In 2015 and 2016, transects were conducted by myself and family members, with family members responsible for spotting and data recording where I was primarily responsible for photography and identification. In 2017, Butterfly Ridge interns were added to the transect activity during the months of June through September.

Table 2 shows our transect data for the year 2015. This data would not be impacted by any habitat work that we would have completed as it normally takes a year for plantings to become established and perennials to begin blooming. Tables 3 through 6 reflect the next four years respectively. These tables show only the total number of butterflies and species for the entire site for each year. Additional tables will reflect habitat and species-specific data.

The number of species recorded throughout the season grew from twenty-seven in 2015 to forty-five in 2019. The increase in species came in two steps. A thirty-three percent increase occurred in 2017. Another approximately thirty-three percent increase came in 2019.

These increases came as a result of maturity within new habitat. In 2015, the Clearing in the East Woods was completed. By 2017 this clearing had matured, with stump sprout black locust gaining in size while native grasses filled the spaces between.

Little wood satyr, which had been absent in the 2015 transect, was not only present, but thriving. Carolina satyr, which had numbered six individuals in 2015, exploded to twenty-five in 2017. These species are dependent on the native grasses within the Clearing.

Silver-spotted skipper, which had numbered six in 2015, exploded to twenty-six in 2017. While these adult skippers were not found in the Clearing, the black locust which was multiplying in the clearing was certainly serving as a nursery for the skippers. Two other species which had not been observed in the Clearing prior to 2017 included pipevine swallowtail and harvester.

Table 2. Transect data for 2015.

Species - 2015	A	M	Jn	Jy	A	S	O
Eastern Comma	4				1		
Mourning Cloak	1						
Gray Hairstreak		1					
Eastern-tailed Blue		2		2	2	6	1
Spring Azure		1					
Dreamy Duskywing		2					
Juvenal's Duskywing		1					
Great Spangled Fritillary			15	3	1	1	
Summer Azure			4		2		
Silver Spotted Skipper			4	1	1		
Spicebush Swallowtail			4		8		
Tawny-edged Skipper			1			2	
Tiger Swallowtail			1		4		
Banded Hairstreak			4				
Red Spotted Purple			1				
Common Wood Nymph				4	2	1	
Pearl Crescent				8		4	1
Tawny Emperor				1	1		
Red Admiral				1			
Common Buckeye				1			
American Lady				1			
Least Skipper					1		
Red-banded Hairsteak					2		
Carolina Satyr					6		
Monarch						1	
Peck's Skipper						2	
Crossline Skipper						1	

Table 3. Transect data for 2016.

Species - 2016	A	M	Jn	Jy	A	S	O
Mourning Cloak				1			
Gray Hairstreak						2	
Eastern-tailed Blue				2	1	10	1
Dreamy Duskywing		7					
Juvenal's Duskywing		6					
Great Spangled Fritillary			1	8	2	5	
Summer Azure						2	
Silver Spotted Skipper			4	2		1	1
Spicebush Swallowtail			3	3	8	2	2
Tiger Swallowtail			2		2	1	
Red Spotted Purple						1	
Common Wood Nymph				2	2		
Pearl Crescent		5		1		3	
Tawny Emperor				1			
American Lady		1	2	1			
Least Skipper			1				
Carolina Satyr		1	1		20	5	
Peck's Skipper			1				
Aphrodite Fritillary				1			
Little Glassywing				2			
Cabbage White					1	1	
Sachem						2	
Cloudless Sulphur							1
Variegated Fritillary							1
Clouded Sulphur							1
Little Wood Satyr			40				

Table 4. Transect data for 2017.

Species - 2017	A	M	Jn	Jy	A	S	O
Eastern Comma	1				1		1
Eastern-tailed Blue		6		1	8	3	2
Spring Azure	2						
Dreamy Duskywing		3					
Juvenal's Duskywing	1	7					
Great Spangled Fritillary			7	5	2	10	
Summer Azure			8	1	2	1	
Silver Spotted Skipper		2	10	5	7	2	
Spicebush Swallowtail		4	7		20	5	1
Tawny-edged Skipper			4				
Tiger Swallowtail		12	2		3	1	
Red Spotted Purple			2				
Common Wood Nymph				1	2	1	
Pearl Crescent		3		3	3	1	4
American Lady		1					1
Least Skipper			1		6		1
Red-banded Hairstreak		3	1		5		
Carolina Satyr					19	6	
Monarch					3	1	
Peck's Skipper			3		2		
Cabbage White			1				
Sachem		1				2	1
Clouded Sulphur			1				
Little Wood Satyr			23				
Eastern Pine Elfin	2						
Zabulon Skipper		2					
Hobomok Skipper		1					
Southern Cloudywing			1				
Pipevine Swallowtail				2			
Dun Skipper			1				
Northern Broken Dash				2		5	
Common Checkered Skipper						1	

Harvester						1	
Orange Sulphur							1
Wild Indigo Duskywing							1
Northern Pearly Eye						1	

Table 5. Transect data for 2018.

Species - 2018	A	M	Jn	Jy	A	S	O
Eastern Comma							9
Gray Hairstreak						1	
Eastern-tailed Blue		3		8		5	3
Dreamy Duskywing		1	3				
Great Spangled Fritillary			1	8	7	1	
Summer Azure					6	2	
Silver Spotted Skipper		1	5	15	18	1	1
Spicebush Swallowtail			7	1	12	1	
Tawny-edged Skipper			6			1	1
Tiger Swallowtail		3	6	1	12	3	
Banded Hairstreak				1			
Red Spotted Purple					2	3	2
Common Wood Nymph				2	2	1	
Pearl Crescent			1	4	3	16	4
Tawny Emperor					1		
Red Admiral							1
Common Buckeye							1
American Lady			3	1			
Least Skipper			6	1	2	4	
Red-banded Hairstreak			3				1
Carolina Satyr			8		41	3	
Monarch				3	5	3	3
Peck's Skipper			6		2		
Little Glassywing			1				
Sachem			1				
Cloudless Sulphur							1
Little Wood Satyr			72				
Southern Cloudywing			4				
Pipevine Swallowtail		2		1			
Dun Skipper						1	
Northern Broken Dash				4	1		
Harvester			1				

Orange Sulphur							2
Horace's Duskywing		1					
Question Mark			1		1	1	3
Hackberry Emperor					1		

Table 6. Transect data for 2019.

Species - 2019	A	M	Jn	Jy	A	S	O
Eastern Comma							7
Gray Hairstreak					1		2
Eastern-tailed Blue				3	24	9	4
Spring Azure		1					
Dreamy Duskywing		1					
Juvenal's Duskywing		1					
Great Spangled Fritillary			5	9	3		
Summer Azure			5		2	1	
Silver Spotted Skipper		1	15	25	31	2	2
Spicebush Swallowtail			10	3	17	4	
Tawny-edged Skipper			4				
Tiger Swallowtail		12	13	1	86	7	
Banded Hairstreak				1			
Red Spotted Purple					1	1	
Common Wood Nymph					2		
Pearl Crescent		11		2	2	28	15
Tawny Emperor				1			
Red Admiral		1	5	1			1
Common Buckeye							2
American Lady		2			4		
Least Skipper			10		9	6	
Red-banded Hairstreak			1				
Carolina Satyr			13		10		
Monarch					8	1	
Peck's Skipper			1	1	1		
Crossline Skipper			1				
Little Glassywing					1		
Cabbage White			1			1	
Cloudless Sulphur						1	

Little Wood Satyr			31			1	
Southern Cloudywing			1				
Zabulon Skipper			1		6		
Pipevine Swallowtail				2			
Dun Skipper					1		
Northern Broken Dash				14			
Harvester			1				
Orange Sulphur				1			1
Wild Indigo Duskywing		1					
Horace's Duskywing					1		
Question Mark					1	1	1
Hackberry Emperor			1		1	1	
Coral Hairstreak				1			
Silvery Checkerspot					3		
Swarthy Skipper					1		
Fiery Skipper						1	
Painted Lady						1	

Another spike in species occurred in 2019. In 2019, the number of species observed on the transects increased from thirty-six to forty-five. This increase was driven largely by new species found in the Prairie, including coral hairstreak, swarthy skipper, zabulon skipper, and fiery skipper. In addition, crossline skipper made an appearance in the tally for 2019 after a four-year absence. Northern broken dash, which had been observed in the Prairie since 2017, experienced a population explosion with fourteen individuals recorded compared to the previous high of seven.

As reminder, the Prairie was created in two phases; a half-acre portion in 2016 and a one-acre portion in 2017. By 2019, both phases had fully matured, with full and vigorous stands of Indian grass and big bluestem complimented with the blooms of native perennials including various milkweeds, bergamot, and mountain mint.

For further evidence of the role that maturation of specific habitats has played we can look at the data from those habitats. Table 7 clearly shows an increase in butterfly activity in the Clearing starting in 2016, one year after this woodland opening was created. The table also shows a twenty percent decline in activity in 2019. This will be further addressed in "The Future" chapter of the book.

Table 7. Individual butterflies tallied from the Clearing habitat.

Clearing	A	M	Jn	Jy	A	S	O	Total
2015	2	4	7	2	10	0	0	25
2016	0	4	11	4	18	12	1	50
2017	0	16	19	0	11	5	1	52
2018	0	5	27	6	14	1	2	55
2019	0	8	18	4	8	3	1	42
Total	2	37	82	16	61	21	5	224

Data from the Prairie (Table 8) shows that butterfly activity showed a modest increase in 2017 with an explosion of activity in 2019. Once again, this reflects maturation of the grasses and perennials found in this habitat. The increased activity in the Prairie is especially pronounced in the summer months of June through August.

Table 8. Individual butterflies tallied in the Prairie habitat.

Prairie	A	M	Jn	Jy	A	S	O	Total
2015	3	3	24	20	18	19	2	89
2016	0	16	42	19	8	23	6	114
2017	5	26	33	17	40	17	9	147
2018	0	6	54	39	44	24	20	187
2019	0	21	58	57	103	41	31	311
Total	8	72	211	152	213	124	68	848

Data from the Checkerboard also reflects the impact of habitat maturation. Work in this habitat began in 2016 with creation of the first woodland opening, an area about one-fourth acre in size. In 2017 two more openings, slightly smaller than the first were created. In 2018 a final woodland opening was created, east of the previous openings but of approximately the same size. No additional openings were created in 2019, although additional openings are planned.

As the data in Table 9 reflects, butterfly activity in the Checkerboard increased markedly in 2018 followed by a decline on 2019. The decline in 2019, while still an increase over the early years of the site, is still troubling and will be addressed in "The Future" chapter of the book.

The significant increase in butterfly activity in 2018 was driven largely by an increase in little wood satyr numbers in June and an equally impressive increase in Carolina satyr in August. The satyrs use the grasses in these openings as their caterpillar host plants.

Table 9. Individual butterflies tallied in the Checkerboard habitat.

Checkerboard	A	M	Jn	Jy	A	S	O	Total
2015	0	0	2	0	1	0	0	3
2016	0	0	2	0	8	0	0	10
2017	0	0	4	0	13	2	0	19
2018	0	0	31	0	28	5	2	66
2019	0	0	18	0	12	4	0	34
Total	0	0	57	0	62	11	2	132

Data from the Wetland shows a similar trend, albeit with a slight caveat. Table 10 shows a slight increase in butterfly activity in 2018 with a massive increase in activity in August 2019. In September, activity returned to normal. In 2018, a few large masses of cup plant (*Silphium perfoliatum*) were planted in the wetland. These plants did not bloom in 2018 but began blooming in late July 2019. These plants proved to be a powerful magnet for swallowtail butterflies. The ninety-one butterflies recorded in August 2019 were almost entirely swallowtails, both tiger and spicebush. The question now begs, was the unusually large number of swallowtails indicative of a great swallowtail year, or did the cup plant have the power to actually attract these swallowtails from a much greater distance than what the previous flora could attract? Time will tell.

Table 10. Butterflies tallied in the Wetland habitat.

Wetland	A	M	Jn	Jy	A	S	O	Total
2017	1	1	14	4	18	18	3	59
2018	0	0	18	6	20	17	8	69
2019	0	2	19	3	91	18	3	136
Total	1	3	51	13	129	53	14	264

While transect data is helpful in giving a glimpse into the butterfly population on our site, it does not provide a complete picture. While we have sixty-three butterfly species on our site list, the best season we have had on the transect was forty-five species in 2019. We have, for example, never had falcate orangetip appear on a transect although in the month of April this species can be relatively common. The problem is that the flight-time of this short-lived butterfly falls between transects. Orangetips tend to emerge after the April transect but are largely deceased by the time the May transect rolls around.

Banded Hairstreak is much the same way. While this species has been represented on the transect regularly, only in 2015 was the population size of this butterfly accurately represented; that year four were recorded.

Normally we will have four to eight banded hairstreaks flying in the Clearing at the same time. However, they normally do not emerge until after the June transect and most have passed prior to the July transect. In 2015, the June transect was conducted on June 7, relatively late in the transect window. In addition, we had experienced a warm spring with May and early June temperatures well into the 80's. Most likely the unseasonably warm temperatures led to an early emergence of this species and our late transect date allowed us to tally these freshly emerged individuals.

Another butterfly that does not appear in the transect data is the American snout. The snout, while not common at Butterfly Ridge, is a regular occurrence in late summer. However, the timing has never quite worked out for this species to appear in the transect data.

The transect data does show encouraging trends for some butterflies. Perhaps one of the most inspiring impacts from our habitat work has been on the pearl crescent. As you can see in Table 11, the pearl crescent made substantial gains in September 2018 and those gains carried through 2019.

The reason for such remarkable gains in pearl crescents is somewhat confusing. In our construction of the Prairie, heath aster, the primary host plant for the pearl crescent, was destroyed, although plenty survives in other fields and some has moved back into the Prairie over time. Additional asters were planted in the new Prairie, largely New England aster, but certainly not enough to offset the loss of the original asters. The most likely explanation for the gains in pearl crescents would probably be the increase in nectar plantings in the Prairie. The additional nectar attracts the pearl crescents, making them more visible for tallying.

Table 11. Pearl Crescent butterflies tallied during transects.

Pearl Crescent	A	M	Jn	Jy	A	S	O	Total
2015				8		4	1	13
2016		5		1		3		9
2017		3		3	3	1	4	14
2018			1	4	3	16	4	28
2019		11		2	2	28	15	58
Total	0	19	1	18	8	52	24	122

The Eastern tiger swallowtail has followed a similar pattern as the pearl crescent, as exemplified in Table 12. Tiger swallowtails on the site began to show a population increase in May 2017 which then exploded in 2019. The caterpillar host plant for the tiger swallowtail in southeast Ohio is the tulip tree. Over the course of habitat creation, we did not add any tulip tree and in fact removed several them from the site.

Table 12. Eastern tiger swallowtail butterflies tallied during transects.

Tiger Swallowtail	A	M	Jn	Jy	A	S	O	Total
2015			1		4			5
2016			2		2	1		5
2017		12	2		3	1		18
2018		3	6	1	12	3		25
2019		12	13	1	86	7		119
Total	0	27	24	2	107	12	0	172

A majority of the additional tiger swallowtail sightings occurred in the Prairie, with the exception of August 2019; these sightings were made in the Wetland. Of course, there is no tulip tree in the Prairie or Wetland, and no additional tulip tree plantings were added adjacent to these habitats.

As was the case with the pearl crescent, I believe the tiger swallowtails were responding to an increased supply of nectar. For this reason, they were able to be spotted for the transect when they normally may had been patrolling treetops. The August 2019 explosion was absolutely in response to the availability of nectar in mass, in this case a new planting of several large masses of cup plant.

A species which grew its population markedly which I think we can attribute to additional host plants is silver-spotted skipper. With the creation of the Clearing, many young black locust trees colonized the habitat. Black locust is the caterpillar host for silver-spotted skipper. The patch of black locust in the Clearing was the densest patch on the property. And, while most skipper sightings were in other habitats, I think many of these skippers began their lives in the Clearing.

As reminder, work in the Clearing was completed in the summer of 2015. As indicated in Table 13, silver-spotted skipper sightings began to increase in 2017 with an explosion of the population in 2018 and 2019.

Table 13. Silver-spotted skipper butterflies tallied during transects.

Silver-spotted Skipper	A	M	Jn	Jy	A	S	O	Total
2015			4	1	1			6
2016			4	2		1	1	8
2017		2	10	5	7	2		26
2018		1	5	15	18	1	1	41
2019		1	15	25	31	2	2	76
Total	0	4	38	48	57	6	4	157

Another species whose population has grown, based largely on an increased number of caterpillar host plants is the eastern comma. The comma uses both elm and nettles as their host plants. While the amount of elm on the property has not changed noticeably, a lot of new false nettle (*Boehmeria cylindrica*) has been planted in the last five years. Most of the new plantings have been added in the Ditch and around the outhouse. In addition, false nettle has begun to naturally spread into the Wetland.

The late summer data for the comma better reflects the overall health of the population. This late generation of the comma overwinters as an adult butterfly, therefore early spring sightings would correspond to the late season sightings from the year before. However, the data in Table 14 does not reflect this correlation. Keep in mind that early spring sightings are extremely weather dependent, and commas that may be present may not be flying to be tallied. In addition, commas are not known for nectaring on flowers, which is another limitation in sighting them on the transect.

Table 14. Eastern comma butterflies tallied during transects.

Eastern Comma	A	M	Jn	Jy	A	S	O	Total
2015	4				1			5
2016								0
2017	1				1		1	3
2018							9	9
2019							7	7
Total	5	0	0	0	2	0	17	24

Another impressive example of the power of planting caterpillar host plants is found in the data relating to the group of butterflies known as the grass skippers. The specific species I have included in this data include crossline skipper, Peck's skipper, least skipper, little glassywing, tawny-edged skipper, hobomok skipper, zabulon skipper, sachem, fiery skipper, and northern broken-dash.

Table 15. Grass skipper butterflies tallied during transects.

Grass Skippers	A	M	Jn	Jy	A	S	O	Total
2015			1		1	5		7
2016			2	2		2		6
2017		4	8	2	8	7	2	31
2018			20	5	5	5	1	36
2019			17	15	18	7		57
Total		4	48	24	32	26	3	137

As displayed in Table 15, the grass skipper population increased markedly in 2017, and again in 2019. Grass skippers use various grasses as their caterpillar host plants. In the planting of the Prairie in 2016 and 2017, roughly twelve pounds of grass seed was used, primarily in the form of big bluestem and Indian grass but also including side-oats grama and little bluestem.

While some of the increase shown in the table could be related to an increase in the availability of nectar plants, thus making the butterflies easier to spot, the increased amount of native grasses in the habitat certainly played a key role as well. Afterall, 2019 shows an eight-fold increase in comparison to 2015.

Transect data that has been collected at Butterfly Ridge, since before habitat alteration started, clearly shows that the habitat work which has been completed has had a powerful, positive influence on the butterfly population at this site. Through the addition of caterpillar host plants and favorable nectar plants, butterflies have absolutely benefitted.

Table 16 shows which species of butterflies are most abundant at Butterfly Ridge, not only for the entire five-year transect history but also specifically for 2019. Eastern tiger swallowtail led the pack in both categories. The table shows that little wood satyr declined in 2019 while eastern tailed-blue had a good year in comparison to the rest of the field. While summer azure took the final spot in the five-year history it did not register as one of the ten most abundant in 2019.

Table 16. Species abundance over the five-year history of the transect compared to 2019 abundance.

Species	All-time rank	2019 rank
Eastern Tiger Swallowtail	1	1
Little Wood Satyr	2	6
Silver-spotted Skipper	3	2
Carolina Satyr	4	8
Spicebush Swallowtail	5	5
Pearl Crescent	5	3
Eastern-tailed Blue	7	4
Great Spangled Fritillary	8	9
Least Skipper	9	7
Summer Azure	10	N/A

10

Moths and Other Organisms

As we have watched the various habitats mature, we have found that other organisms have taken advantage of our work as well. In the summer of 2019, we had large swarms of dragonflies flying throughout the prairie, undoubtedly hunting other insects. We have also had a diverse collection of planthoppers, bees, and flies observed, both day and night on site. Most of our observations have been anecdotal, not backed up with data in any way, but we have lots of photos of the other forms of wildlife who call Butterfly Ridge home and we are hopeful that we can develop a more formal data collection tool for these other organisms.

One group of organisms that we have been able to collect data from are the moths. My father and I began moth lighting at what would become Butterfly Ridge in the summer of 2015. We used a homemade scaffolding of one-inch pvc pipe. We hung a sheet in the middle of the scaffolding with a mercury vapor light on one side of the sheet and an ultraviolet light on the other side. All of this was plugged into the garage of our home.

While we did not keep strict counts of the moths that came to the sheet during these times, we did keep a running tally of species observed. In 2017, using the same pvc scaffolding, this time operated with the aid of small Honda generator, we opened the moth lighting to the public and began setting up the lights in different locations of the Butterfly Ridge property.

In 2019, after some problems with wind wreaking havoc with the portable mothing stations, we created permanent mothing stations at seven locations along the trail and in a variety of different habitats. We placed stations in the Wetland, Checkerboard, Clearing, Prairie, Homestead Loop, a wooded edge between the Clearing and the East Woods, and a woodland opening between the South Woods and the adjacent pine grove (see Figure 24). The new stations work off the same principle as the portable units, with a sheet hanging in the middle, mercury vapor light on one side and ultraviolet light on the other side, all powered by the Honda generator.

In spring of 2018 our moth list was comprised of 330 species. As of the end of the 2019 mothing season, our list totaled 510 species with more than 100 species being added during the 2019 season.

Figure 22. Portable moth lighting scaffolding.

Figure 23. Permanent mothing stations erected in 2019.

The Prairie is most productive of the habitats, with warm summer nights generating a massive number of moths visiting the sheet. On a July night in 2019, the Prairie sheet yielded seven different species of sphinx moths and 123 species of moths total, which is an outstanding species total for southeast Ohio.

In the spring, the mothing station near the family home is very productive. While this sheet is in the front yard, forest, fruit trees, and early successional habitats are all nearby. On May 24, 2019, fifty-eight species were tallied at this location. While this is considerably less than the Prairie totals, it is important to note that the actual number of individual moths in the front yard was much higher. For example, over one hundred hickory tussock moths have been documented at the front yard station on a single May evening.

Figure 24. Locations of permanent mothing stations.

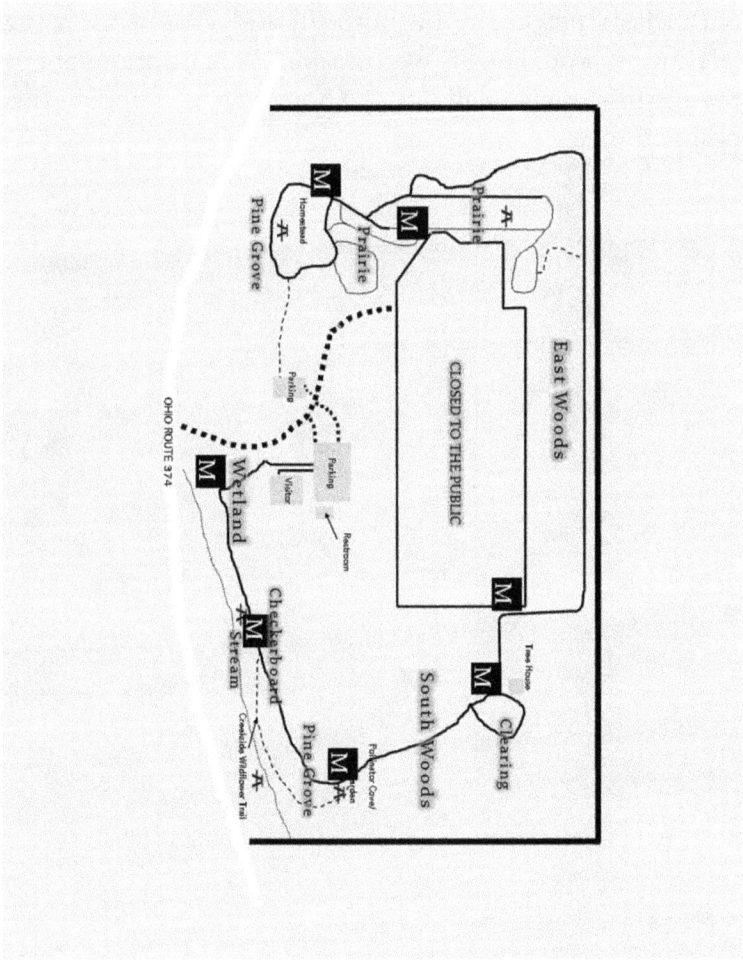

While mothing at the other locations of the property have yielded habitat specific moths, the most diverse, abundant, and productive lighting have taken place in the prairie and in front of our home.

One of our frequent Butterfly Ridge visitors and moth enthusiasts has created a Butterfly Ridge project on the iNaturalist web site. As we continue to learn more about the organisms that call our site home, we will update this online project.

.

Part Four

Moving Forward

11

The Future

As we have studied the transect data that has been gathered for five years, there are certain things that stand out as needing attention. In the future, we will make some adjustments to our habitat work in response to this data.

One of the adjustments that will be made relates directly to the Clearing. As we look at the data, we find that the population of little wood satyrs and Carolina satyrs peaked in 2018 and then experienced a downturn in 2019.

We think that perhaps the black locust which has colonized the Clearing has created a limitation for these satyrs by displacing the caterpillar host grasses that the satyrs utilize. In response, in 2020 a concerted effort will be made to decrease the number of black locust trees that occupy the clearing. As we do this it will be important to monitor the population of silver spotted skippers, the butterfly that uses the black locust as a caterpillar host.

Trying to find a balance between the satyrs and the skippers will be critical.

Table 17. Little wood satyr butterflies tallied during transects.

Little Wood Satyr	A	M	Jn	Jy	A	S	O	Total
2015								0
2016			40					40
2017			23					23
2018			72					72
2019			31			1		32
Total	0	0	166	0	0	1	0	167

Table 18. Carolina satyr butterflies tallied during transects.

Carolina Satyr	A	M	Jn	Jy	A	S	O	Total
2015						6		6
2016		1	1		20	5		27
2017					19	6		25
2018			8		41	3		52
2019			13		10			23
Total	0	1	22	0	90	20	0	133

While much of our work is done on a large scale, there will be plenty of future small-scale projects. Additions will be made to the Prairie around the edges, with 1000 square foot patches of old field and early successional habitat being converted to prairie.

In the existing sections of prairie, additional perennial wildflowers will be added over time. Our initial planting of the Prairie was too heavy in grasses. Late June and July when the bergamot and mountain mint blooms, the floral display in the Prairie is quite impressive. However, prior to that, flowering in the Prairie is limited largely to downy wood-mint and butterfly weed. After July, flowering in this habitat is present but rather spotty, limited to isolated blazing stars, thistles, and late-flowering boneset. Using the hand operated rototiller, we will replant 100 square foot sections of the Prairie with an emphasis on native perennial wildflowers and short prairie grasses.

Another habitat needing future attention will be the Checkerboard. At least two more woodland openings will be added to this area. Here, concerted efforts will be made to prevent any tree species from colonizing these openings, a slightly different approach than what we have taken in the Clearing. By doing so, we can better guarantee future habitat for satyr butterflies.

A habitat that has not been addressed thus far in this book is the different sections of pine forest. We have two pine groves on the property; one adjacent to the Homestead Loop, the other adjacent to the Checkerboard. The latter pine grove is threatened by the encroachment of deciduous tree species. In the last two years we have slowly worked on removing deciduous trees from this grove. We have begun transplanting pine seedlings that colonize the fields adjacent to the Prairie into this pine grove. We will continue the work of removing deciduous trees from both pine groves and planting young pines in the Checkerboard pine grove.

Figure 27. Locations of pine groves at Butterfly Ridge.

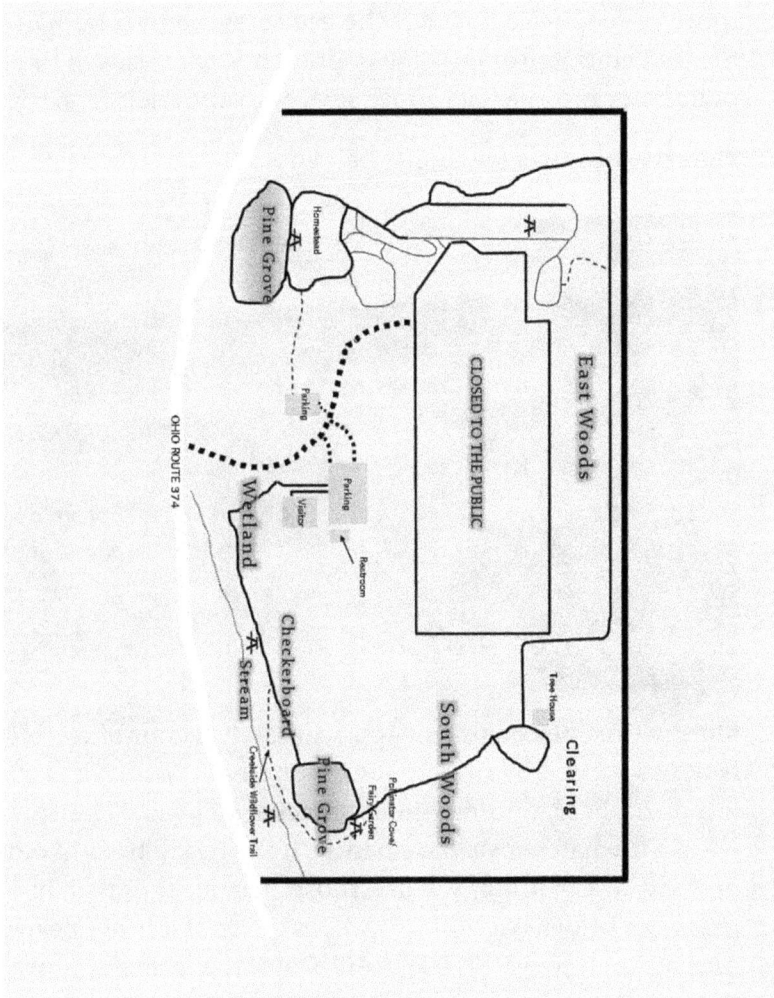

A final future project, which should be relatively easy to accomplish, is the creation of more bait stations for our tree sap/rotten fruit feeding butterflies. Our bait stations consist of a stick of firewood with two eye screws in the top. We feed wire through the eye screws and then hang the bait station from the lower branches of trees. We then pour bait onto the flat, upper surface of the stick.

Figure 28. Insects feeding at bait stick.

Our bait recipe consists of approximately 2 cups of rotting fruit, two cups of brown sugar, one-half bottle of dark imported beer, and one-fourth packet of yeast. The fruit we use is whatever we have handy. If the peach trees in our orchard are fruiting, we use those, letting them sit in a plastic or brown bags for two weeks to rot. If it is not peach season then we will use fruit from the grocery store, normally either bananas or plums, which we then allow to rot.

We went through a period in 2019 when the bait was not attracting butterflies. We contacted Marianna Trevino-Wright, director of the National Butterfly Center in Mission, Texas, for advice and she suggested adding the yeast, to allow the mixture to "cook" further. The addition of yeast had an immediate positive impact.

The reason we specifically use dark, imported beer is not solely because it is my favorite! Butterflies prefer the dark beers and the imported beers do not require pasteurization, once again allowing fermentation to continue a little longer. The reason beer is added to the mixture at all is to simulate the fermentation of the rotting fruit that the butterflies so much enjoy.

One negative aspect of the bait stick is that it also attracts other insects, especially yellow jackets and bald-faced hornets. While the bees do occasionally try to chase the butterflies away from the bait, we have never had occasion where the bees became aggressive with humans watching or photographing the activity at the bait stick.

In addition to the bait stick providing necessary nutrition to our fruit feeding butterflies, especially eastern commas, question marks, red admirals, and emperors, the bait sticks also preoccupy the butterflies, making them easier to tally during transect walks. We are hopeful that additional bait sticks will help us get an even more accurate picture of our butterfly populations.

12

Starting Your Own Butterfly Habitat

As I was driving across the country recently, I began looking at the landscape differently than I had before. As I drove, an amazing, but totally unrealistic, idea crossed my mind. I imagined how fun it would be to purchase twenty acres of land in every state of the United States and develop a Butterfly Ridge there. Can you imagine, fifty Butterfly Ridges across the country?

Of course, financially this is totally unrealistic. My cash flow is nowhere near liquid enough to afford something like this. Also, when you consider we currently have five years invested in Butterfly Ridge (Ohio), five years times forty-nine states is more time than I probably have left. Perhaps I could accomplish my goal vicariously through other butterfly enthusiasts however; no franchise fees or anything! I am sure I could get some takers to my idea, but my hunch is that they would all have the same initial question, "Where do I start?"

Getting started requires two major research projects. The first is to determine which butterflies are already on your site, or within a few miles of your site. This is important for a couple reasons. The butterflies that you already have will dictate which plants you plant. For example, it would be silly for me to plant wild columbine at Butterfly Ridge to attract columbine duskywing when the closest sightings of this butterfly are nearly 200 miles away. Of course, we have planted wild columbine, but we have done so to add spring color to our trails, not to attract this butterfly.

Along these same lines it is important to accept that if you are butterfly gardening in an urban landscape, especially within a large metropolitan area, your pool of potential butterfly species to attract is going to be quite limited. Do not let this stop you, however. Yes, you may have only five butterfly species in your area, but you can have a magical Shangri-La for those five, nonetheless.

Once you have determined which butterfly species you have in your area, you then need to research the caterpillar host plants for those butterflies. These are the plants that the butterflies will lay eggs upon and will be the focus of your initial plantings. Of course, you want these plants to be native to your area. Native species are naturally suited for your local environment. They will require less watering, winterizing, and other care. Plus, the local butterflies have utilized the local natives for hundreds of generations; it is a known entity.

Native nectar plants are also an important consideration. While many caterpillar host plants also serve as good nectar, it is not a guarantee. False nettle (*Boehmeria cylindrica*) for example is an excellent host plant for red admiral and question mark butterflies but offers no nectar value whatsoever. As a rule, any members of the milkweed, mint, and sunflower family can be assumed to be a good nectar plant.

In areas that do not have a strong native nectar flora, garden annuals can be used to supplement the native nectar sources. The annuals that seem to be best suited for butterflies include lantana, French marigolds, zinnia, and cosmos. Despite what some people consider as factual, annuals like petunias, snapdragons, and begonias are not strong butterfly nectar plants. The reason is simple; butterflies prefer flowers that are tubular shaped, with several flowers clustered together. Lantana provides the perfect example of this flower structure. Petunias, with their large, bell-shaped flowers, do not have the structure which butterflies need.

Additional research will include finding sources for the plants you need. Perhaps the simplest route would be to follow in Butterfly Ridge's footsteps and grow plant material from seed. Hopefully much of the seed can be gathered from your own site or nearby. If local seed is not available, then online seed sources can usually be found. Purchasing plants to stock your site can be cost prohibitive, especially if your project will be larger than a residential lot.

Another source for seeds is your friends and neighbors. As example, we started a Facebook page seed exchange. In our exchange, fellow Ohioans can trade seed back and forth to acquire new plant species that may be native to the area but not necessarily to their site.

What I thought I would do is provide a couple of examples of how I would get started in different areas of the country. Hopefully this will give you some ideas of how to get started on your own property.

Kansas

Prior to the encroachment of livestock and agriculture, Kansas would have been a natural butterfly Shangri-La. The mix of prairie grasses and perennial wildflowers would have provided the perfect butterfly garden. However, with the introduction of intensive agriculture, the native seed bank was destroyed by plowing, tilling, and herbicide use. The trampling of plants and soils by livestock hooves disturbed rich soils, creating a breeding grounds for exotic plant species that thrive on disturbance.

To start a Butterfly Ridge in Kansas would be a simple strategy; take the land back to what it once was. While the strategy would be simple, the implementation would require much the same work that we did to create our Butterfly Ridge in Ohio. The first step, through discing and repeated tilling, would be to remove the agricultural and exotic plants that replaced the original prairie. Following this exotic removal, the next step would be to reseed the area with the plant species that had once thrived on the High Plains.

An important maintenance priority for large-scale butterfly habitat creation in not only Kansas but throughout the west and central plains, is the control of livestock wandering in from adjacent properties. Grazing laws in the United States do not require livestock to be fenced in, but rather fenced out. Make sure strong fences are deployed around the habitat to prevent grazing or trampling of your work.

As I traveled across Texas another impact of grazing struck my mind. Passing an area near Van Horn, Texas, signs posted along the highway announced that the property was for sale; $16,000 for 20 acres. I thought it rather ironic that I encountered this sign as I was thinking about my grandiose dream butterfly habitat everywhere. The downside of the property was that it had obviously been grazed, hard. The entire flora consisted of creosote bush, stationed roughly 20 feet apart from each other. The flora across the fence along the highway right of way included a multitude of grass, forbs, mesquite, and creosote. As you can see, one of the challenges of creating habitat in cattle grazing country is not only preventing the cattle from grazing on your habitat, but also repairing the damage from past, irresponsible grazing.

Arizona/New Mexico

I love the mid-elevation areas of the desert southwest for butterfly exploring. The flora of these areas covers a wide range of plant families which makes them ideal for butterflies. Juniper would attract juniper hairstreak and agave would attract giant skippers. The native grasses would attract various grass skippers and satyrs. Native buckwheats would attract blues and hairstreaks.

In this area, native nectar may be a little harder to come by. Native members of the sunflower and legume families would probably be the best choice however some supplemental annuals may be necessary to provide adequate nectar.

In this environment, getting plants established may also prove more difficult due to lack of precipitation. Supplemental watering may also be required to a degree. With this in mind, development of a water harvesting system would be beneficial. At Butterfly Ridge, we have six, 160-gallon rain barrels attached to the down spouting of our home and various outbuildings. In the over 4000 plants we have grown from seed since 2015, none of them have ever received a drop of well water.

In addition, a simple drip irrigation system could be attached directly to a rain barrel system. Electricity would be required to operate the timer on an automatic drip system, or perhaps use a simple portable solar generator to operate the timer. We have built two portable solar generators from an instruction manual purchased from Blue Rock Station Green Living Center in Philo, Ohio.

As you can see, developing butterfly habitat on a large (or small) scale is not rocket science. It requires a little bit of research identifying your local butterflies and the plants they utilize and then a dedication to making it happen.

Appendix A

Additional Butterfly Species Transect Tables

Azure, Spring	A	M	Jn	Jy	A	S	O	Total
2015		1						1
2016								0
2017	2							2
2018								0
2019		1						1
Total	2	2	0	0	0	0	0	4

Azure, Summer	A	M	Jn	Jy	A	S	O	Total
2015			4		2			6
2016						2		2
2017			8	1	2	1		12
2018					6	2		8
2019			5		2	1		8
Total	0	0	17	1	12	6	0	36

Blue, Eastern-tailed	A	M	Jn	Jy	A	S	O	Total
2015		2		2	2	6	1	13
2016				2	1	10	1	14
2017		6		1	8	3	2	20
2018		3		8		5	3	19
2019				3	24	9	4	40
Total	0	11	0	16	35	33	11	106

Buckeye, Common	A	M	Jn	Jy	A	S	O	Total
2015				1				1
2016								0
2017								0
2018							1	1
2019							2	2
Total	0	0	0	1	0	0	3	4

Checkerspot, Silvery	A	M	Jn	Jy	A	S	O	Total
2015								0
2016								0
2017								0
2018								0
2019					3			3
Total	0	0	0	0	3	0	0	3

Comma, Eastern	A	M	Jn	Jy	A	S	O	Total
2015	4				1			5
2016								0
2017	1				1		1	3
2018							9	9
2019							7	7
Total	5	0	0	0	2	0	17	24

Common Wood Nymph	A	M	Jn	Jy	A	S	O	Total
2015				4	2	1		7
2016				2	2			4
2017				1	2	1		4
2018				2	2	1		5
2019					2			2
Total	0	0	0	9	10	3	0	22

Crescent, Pearl	A	M	Jn	Jy	A	S	O	Total
2015				8		4	1	13
2016		5		1		3		9
2017		3		3	3	1	4	14
2018			1	4	3	16	4	28
2019		11		2	2	28	15	58
Total	0	19	1	18	8	52	24	122

Dash, Northern Broken	A	M	Jn	Jy	A	S	O	Total
2015								0
2016								0
2017				2		5		7
2018				4	1			5
2019				14				14
Total	0	0	0	20	1	5	0	26

Duskywing, Dreamy	A	M	Jn	Jy	A	S	O	Total
2015		2						2
2016		7						7
2017		3						3
2018		1	3					4
2019		1						1
Total	0	14	3	0	0	0	0	17

Duskywing, Horace's	A	M	Jn	Jy	A	S	O	Total
2015								0
2016								0
2017								0
2018		1						1
2019					1			1
Total	0	1	0	0	1	0	0	2

Duskywing, Juvenal's	A	M	Jn	Jy	A	S	O	Total
2015		1						1
2016		6						6
2017	1	7						8
2018								0
2019		1						1
Total	1	15	0	0	0	0	0	16

Elfin, Eastern Pine	A	M	Jn	Jy	A	S	O	Total
2015								0
2016								0
2017	2							2
2018								0
2019								0
Total	2	0	0	0	0	0	0	2

Emperor, Hackberry	A	M	Jn	Jy	A	S	O	Total
2015								0
2016								0
2017								0
2018					1			1
2019			1		1	1		3
Total	0	0	1	0	2	1	0	4

Emperor, Tawny	A	M	Jn	Jy	A	S	O	Total
2015				1	1			2
2016				1				1
2017								0
2018					1			1
2019				1				1
Total	0	0	0	3	2	0	0	5

Fritillary, Aphrodite	A	M	Jn	Jy	A	S	O	Total
2015								0
2016				1				1
2017								0
2018								0
2019								0
Total	0	0	0	1	0	0	0	1

Fritillary, Great Spangled	A	M	Jn	Jy	A	S	O	Total
2015			15	3	1	1		20
2016			1	8	2	5		16
2017			7	5	2	10		24
2018			1	8	7	1		17
2019			5	9	3			17
Total	0	0	29	33	15	17	0	94

Fritillary, Variegated	A	M	Jn	Jy	A	S	O	Total
2015								0
2016							1	1
2017								0
2018								0
2019								0
Total	0	0	0	0	0	0	1	1

Hairstreak, Banded	A	M	Jn	Jy	A	S	O	Total
2015			4					4
2016								0
2017								0
2018				1				1
2019				1				1
Total	0	0	4	2	0	0	0	6

Hairstreak, Coral	A	M	Jn	Jy	A	S	O	Total
2015								0
2016								0
2017								0
2018								0
2019				1				1
Total	0	0	0	1	0	0	0	1

Hairstreak, Gray	A	M	Jn	Jy	A	S	O	Total
2015		1						1
2016						2		2
2017								0
2018						1		1
2019					1		2	3
Total	0	1	0	0	1	3	2	7

Hairstreak, Red-banded	A	M	Jn	Jy	A	S	O	Total
2015					2			2
2016								0
2017		3	1		5			9
2018			3				1	4
2019			1					1
Total	0	3	5	0	7	0	1	16

Harvester	A	M	Jn	Jy	A	S	O	Total
2015								0
2016								0
2017						1		1
2018			1					1
2019			1					1
Total	0	0	2	0	0	1	0	3

Lady, American	A	M	Jn	Jy	A	S	O	Total
2015				1				1
2016		1	2	1				4
2017		1					1	2
2018			3	1				4
2019		2			4			6
Total	0	4	5	3	4	0	1	17

Lady, Painted	A	M	Jn	Jy	A	S	O	Total
2015								0
2016								0
2017								0
2018								0
2019						1		1
Total	0	0	0	0	0	1	0	1

Little Glassywing	A	M	Jn	Jy	A	S	O	Total
2015								0
2016				2				2
2017								0
2018			1					1
2019					1			1
Total	0	0	1	2	1	0	0	4

Monarch	A	M	Jn	Jy	A	S	O	Total
2015						1		1
2016								0
2017					3	1		4
2018				3	5	3	3	14
2019					8	1		9
Total	0	0	0	3	16	6	3	28

Mourning Cloak	A	M	Jn	Jy	A	S	O	Total
2015	1							1
2016				1				1
2017								0
2018								0
2019								0
Total	1	0	0	1	0	0	0	2

Red Admiral	A	M	Jn	Jy	A	S	O	Total
2015				1				1
2016								0
2017								0
2018							1	1
2019		1	5	1			1	8
Total	0	1	5	2	0	0	2	10

Red spotted Purple	A	M	Jn	Jy	A	S	O	Total
2015			1					1
2016						1		1
2017			2					2
2018					2	3	2	7
2019					1	1		2
Total	0	0	3	0	3	5	2	13

Sachem	A	M	Jn	Jy	A	S	O	Total
2015								0
2016						2		2
2017		1				2	1	4
2018			1					1
2019								0
Total	0	1	1	0	0	4	1	7

Satyr, Carolina	A	M	Jn	Jy	A	S	O	Total
2015						6		6
2016		1	1		20	5		27
2017					19	6		25
2018			8		41	3		52
2019			13		10			23
Total	0	1	22	0	90	20	0	133

Satyr, Little Wood	A	M	Jn	Jy	A	S	O	Total
2015								0
2016			40					40
2017			23					23
2018			72					72
2019			31			1		32
Total	0	0	166	0	0	1	0	167

Skipper, Common Checkered	A	M	Jn	Jy	A	S	O	Total
2015								0
2016								0
2017						1		1
2018								0
2019								0
Total	0	0	0	0	0	1	0	1

Skipper, Crossline	A	M	Jn	Jy	A	S	O	Total
2015						1		1
2016								0
2017								0
2018								0
2019			1					1
Total	0	0	1	0	0	1	0	2

Skipper, Dun	A	M	Jn	Jy	A	S	O	Total
2015								0
2016								0
2017			1					1
2018						1		1
2019					1			1
Total	0	0	1	0	1	1	0	3

Skipper, Fiery	A	M	Jn	Jy	A	S	O	Total
2015								0
2016								0
2017								0
2018								0
2019						1		1
Total	0	0	0	0	0	1	0	1

Skipper, Hobomok	A	M	Jn	Jy	A	S	O	Total
2015								0
2016								0
2017		1						1
2018								0
2019								0
Total	0	1	0	0	0	0	0	1

Skipper, Least	A	M	Jn	Jy	A	S	O	Total
2015					1			1
2016			1					1
2017			1		6		1	8
2018			6	1	2	4		13
2019			10		9	6		25
Total	0	0	18	1	18	10	1	48

Skipper, Pecks	A	M	Jn	Jy	A	S	O	Total
2015						2		2
2016			1					1
2017			3		2			5
2018			6		2			8
2019			1	1	1			3
Total	0	0	11	1	5	2	0	19

Skipper, Silver-spotted	A	M	Jn	Jy	A	S	O	Total
2015			4	1	1			6
2016			4	2		1	1	8
2017		2	10	5	7	2		26
2018		1	5	15	18	1	1	41
2019		1	15	25	31	2	2	76
Total	0	4	38	48	57	6	4	157

Skipper, Swarthy	A	M	Jn	Jy	A	S	O	Total
2015								0
2016								0
2017								0
2018								0
2019					1			1
Total	0	0	0	0	1	0	0	1

Skipper, Tawny-edged	A	M	Jn	Jy	A	S	O	Total
2015			1			2		3
2016								0
2017			4					4
2018			6			1	1	8
2019			4					4
Total	0	0	15	0	0	3	1	19

Skipper, Zabulon	A	M	Jn	Jy	A	S	O	Total
2015								0
2016								0
2017		2						2
2018								0
2019			1		6			7
Total	0	2	1	0	6	0	0	9

Sulphur, Clouded	A	M	Jn	Jy	A	S	O	Total
2015								0
2016							1	1
2017			1					1
2018								0
2019								0
Total	0	0	1	0	0	0	1	2

Sulphur, Cloudless	A	M	Jn	Jy	A	S	O	Total
2015								0
2016							1	1
2017								0
2018							1	1
2019						1		1
Total	0	0	0	0	0	1	2	3

Sulphur, Orange	A	M	Jn	Jy	A	S	O	Total
2015								0
2016								0
2017							1	1
2018							2	2
2019				1			1	2
Total	0	0	0	1	0	0	4	5

Swallowtail, Eastern Tiger	A	M	Jn	Jy	A	S	O	Total
2015			1		4			5
2016			2		2	1		5
2017		12	2		3	1		18
2018		3	6	1	12	3		25
2019		12	13	1	86	7		119
Total	0	27	24	2	107	12	0	172

Swallowtail, Pipevine	A	M	Jn	Jy	A	S	O	Total
2015								0
2016								0
2017				2				2
2018		2		1				3
2019				2				2
Total	0	2	0	5	0	0	0	7

Swallowtail, Spicebush	A	M	Jn	Jy	A	S	O	Total
2015			4		8			12
2016			3	3	8	2	2	18
2017		4	7		20	5	1	37
2018			7	1	12	1		21
2019			10	3	17	4		34
Total	0	4	31	7	65	12	3	122

White, Cabbage	A	M	Jn	Jy	A	S	O	Total
2015								
2016					1	1		2
2017			1					1
2018								0
2019			1			1		2
Total	0	0	2	0	1	2	0	5

www.ingramcontent.com/pod-product-compliance
Lightning Source LLC
Chambersburg PA
CBHW050734030426
42336CB00012B/1562